T0114894

L'DOR V'DOR:
GENERATION TO GENERATION

SUCCESSION PLANNING IN FAMILY BUSINESSES:
OWNERS' PERCEPTIONS AND PRACTICES

MATTHEW R. KERZNER, PH.D.

authorHOUSE

AuthorHouse™
1663 Liberty Drive
Bloomington, IN 47403
www.authorhouse.com
Phone: 833-262-8899

© 2023 Matthew R. Kerzner, Ph.D. All rights reserved.

No part of this book may be reproduced, stored in a retrieval system, or
transmitted by any means without the written permission of the author.

Published by AuthorHouse 06/21/2023

ISBN: 979-8-8230-1034-4 (sc)
ISBN: 979-8-8230-1033-7 (e)

Library of Congress Control Number: 2023911311

Print information available on the last page.

Any people depicted in stock imagery provided by Getty Images are models,
and such images are being used for illustrative purposes only.
Certain stock imagery © Getty Images.

This book is printed on acid-free paper.

Because of the dynamic nature of the Internet, any web addresses or links contained in
this book may have changed since publication and may no longer be valid. The views
expressed in this work are solely those of the author and do not necessarily reflect the
views of the publisher, and the publisher hereby disclaims any responsibility for them.

CONTENTS

FOREWORD

By Lisë Stewart, Partner Eisner Advisory Group LLC

The room was small and bright, but stuffy. The two brothers, Ted and Terry, co-owners and leaders of their third-generation company, were struggling to tell their story. One brother was slow to speak, taking a long time to form his thoughts and meandering his way through a torturous story. The older brother was talking quickly, his thoughts rushing out as he constantly interrupted Terry. Each time he interrupted, he'd apologize quickly and then do it again. We could see that this was hard, and progress would be slow. These two men had some difficult decisions to make, and they simply were not aligned. After fifteen minutes of assessing the situation, Matt cleared his throat and checked to see if he could ask a few questions. At first, the older brother looked alarmed at being stopped mid-stream, but Matt has an affable style, so it's hard not to agree.

"I'm really curious about the history of the company... can you tell me about..." And, so it began, the conversation turn-around. It was lovely to see Matt in full family business advisor mode – deftly asking questions, making it easy for the brothers to respond, hitting upon topics that obviously had a lot of history and meaning. After a while, he transitioned to questions about today... getting important details about the current state. Finally, he alluded to the next step in the process, fleshing out the future. At this point, one might say, 'Well of course, any good family business advisor does that," and you'd be right, except for the STAMP. The Kerzner STAMP captures not only a methodology, but a philosophy. What makes this philosophy and the associated process unique? It is the foundation of understanding, empathy, rigor, and commitment that underpins that list of seemingly simple questions.

I have been working with family businesses for over 30 years and have trained hundreds of family business consultants in the art of working with families who own and operate businesses. In all of these years, I have learned some simple, but unshakable truths: compassion and respect for what the family, and particularly family business leaders are experiencing, sacrificing, and developing are key to the success of the relationship and engagement. We must balance family needs with business needs because when things get really tough and hard decisions need to be made, the family needs will almost always take precedence. Any consultant who focuses on just one or the other will do both the family and the business a serious disservice.

The past, present, and future all matter. It is tempting to try to push the family to focus on the future, to make improvements and to be strategic. However, all families share a common history and the experiences and values of that shared legacy have a significant, if not always recognized, impact on the present and the future. When we honor the past, we open doors of understanding for the future.

Questions are the key. It is so tempting for advisors to enter into the relationship with their family business clients by trying to 'tell' the client why they are so smart, special, talented, important, and worth the money that they will be paid. However, the most important thing a skilled advisor can do is to ask a few powerful questions and then be quiet, and really listen. Listen beyond the words. Search for meaning, look for cues, pay attention to the whole, gently probe for more information. And, finally, back it all up with solid research – a clear understanding of processes, methodologies, ways to make and then test assumptions. This is an ever-changing and growing field, and advisors must stay active in their own learning to remain effective.

This is why I am pleased to offer my enthusiastic recommendation for this book and its body of knowledge. Matt is sharing tools, techniques, illustrative stories, and personal anecdotes that have become the hallmark of his success as a skilled advisor. His Kerzner STAMP brings his methodology to life by providing families and advisors with a simple tool for understanding what was, what is, and what might be.

If you are a family business owner or working in a family business, this book provides a series of important steps to take to understand your business and its potential, your culture, and methods for sustaining and/or transforming your company through effective succession and transition strategies. If you are an advisor to a family business, this book will become a trusted guide – a reference for ensuring your ability to utilize current research, proven techniques, and common sense to bring the best of services to your clients.

Working with a family business is a journey built upon mutual trust, a commitment to learn and change, and a willingness to be vulnerable, challenged, and fully engaged. I am thankful to Matt and our clients and our shared projects for allowing me to be all of that and more. I am grateful that he has given you, the reader, the opportunity to join the journey.

INTRODUCTION

MY FATHER'S STORY

MiKERZ and Cousin Robert in delivery car

I can still remember my father, Michael Kerzner, standing behind the counter of MiKERZ Pharmacy, a business he started in 1967 and sold in 1988. With his steadfast work ethic, unswerving stamina, and unique knowledge of every customer, my father was the epitome of a true businessman. And in his pharmacy, prescriptions were more than just prescriptions. There was a story behind each medicine, and my father's customers literally trusted him with their lives. If a customer was sent home from a physician or released from the hospital, my father was called first. Yes, of course, their prescriptions needed to be filled, but it was my dad's genuine bedside manner that was also sought and much appreciated.

My father was an integral part and presence of his neighborhood. He was the #1 Pharmacist in Waterbury, CT, and he delivered to the four corners of that city. My grandfather did the books for the store, and numerous family members, including my three siblings, cousins, and myself, worked there, too. Whether it was preparing third-party billing, doing the accounting, working the retail end, or delivering prescriptions, we all felt we had contributed to the success of this business. It was a true "generation-to-generation" establishment. I smile when I think of how I put on my suit and tie as a 10-year-old because I knew "going to work" was more than just "going to work". I would dust and sweep and follow my dad around the pharmacy. More importantly, I watched my dad make connections and care about the community. With the combination of his intense concentration and that smirk of satisfaction, my father was proud of the business he built. I watched him become the captain of his own ship, and I watched my family support him to do just that. I knew at that early age that I would always work hard, strive to improve, and be the best I could be. I also knew I wanted, and needed, to understand family business.

Dad in his youth behind counter

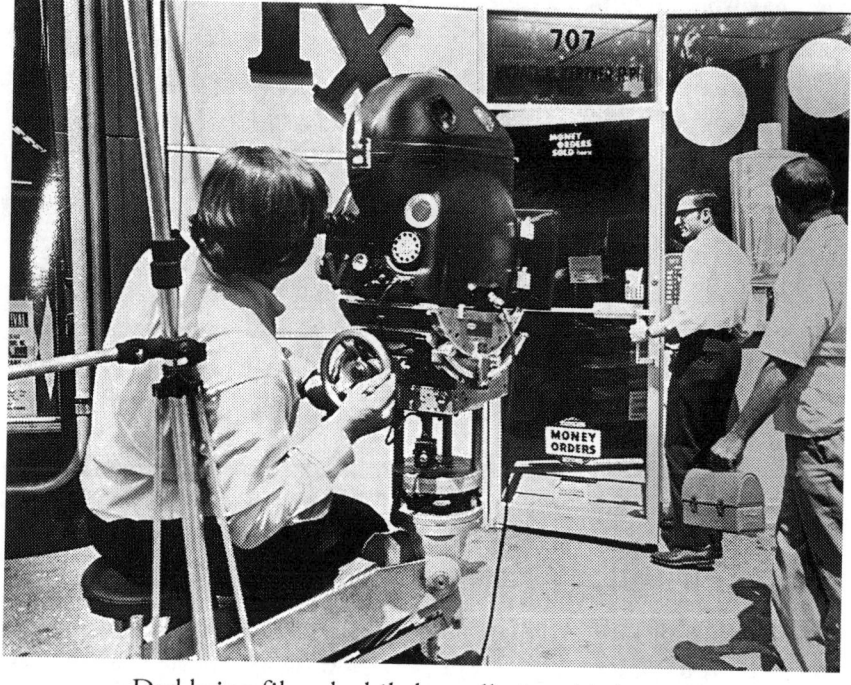

Dad being filmed while he walks into his business

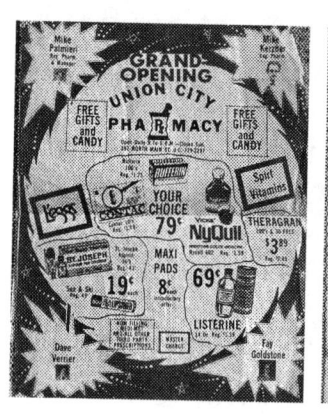

Grand opening announcements

In the years that he was standing behind the counter filling prescriptions, my father acquired two additional pharmacies, David's Union City and Nelsons. Over the years, he also bought Spirit Vitamin Company and Medical Equipment Unlimited. He eventually sold Nelsons to his general manager and Medical Equipment Unlimited to his successor, carrying out his successions within his own businesses. Because my father did not have any family members with a desire to go into the Pharmacy trade, he sold MiKERZ Pharmacy to an exceptionally large food retail operation, Stop & Shop. Little did I know that that business would play a significant role in my future pursuits of becoming a human resource expert and an industrial organizational business psychologist.

Without question, I learned so many valuable lessons over the years, both working for my dad as well as using him as a mentor and sounding board for all my goals and dreams. My father knew how to balance ownership, family, and business. An honorable man, my dad knew that customer service was his number one priority. He also knew that hard work was the foundation to a happy life, and that it took a team to get there. He was blessed because he had both. My father also knew that it was important to support the community and give back, a principle he instilled in my siblings and me. Finally, he knew the importance of "generation to generation" in business, and he knew when to get out, as that was his succession plan.

My father was a devoted entrepreneur and business owner who not only took care of his customers but also the community he served. Although I did not wish to follow in his footsteps of becoming a pharmacist, I had his passion for the innerworkings of a business. I still wanted to better understand the succession planning process and how family business owners worked out their succession plan. There were so many questions that I wanted answered: How did business owners think about their families, their employees, and their communities? How did the owners, especially second-generation ones, honor their past, while having a good awareness of their present state? And how did they think about their future? Were they passing the business to the next generation, or was selling the business part of their plan? That is the reason I wanted to tell my story and write this book. Now, 35 years later as I am writing about succession planning, I know my father is looking down and smiling with pride. He knows that I am honoring the past, he is watching me succeed in the present, and he is guiding me through the lessons I learned to help me be the best I can be in the future. L'Dor V'dor.

Your Time to Reflect:

- *Do you have a story? Have you told it to anyone? If yes, what happened when you did? If not, why not?*
- *Create a list of some of your passions*
- *What dreams do you imagine? What questions keep you up at night? How do you find the answers? To whom do you turn?*
- *How has your past helped to shape your present and your future?*

CHAPTER 1

MY JOURNEY

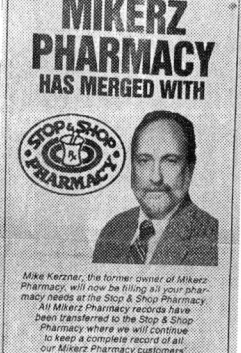

Original Stop and Shop, MiKERZ Pharmacy Merger,
Matt working store operations at the age of 23

With a passion for both psychology and business systems, I earned
my industrial organizational psychology degree from Nichols College.
Upon graduation and not having a family business to run or manage,
I followed my father's path of taking a job with Stop and Shop, the
food retail operation my father sold his business to, and I entered their
management training program. I was 23 years old at this time. After
an 18-month training program, I started my journey of learning big
business, and this was the time my fascination with succession planning
started to grow. Being part of a pilot program to help fill the need of
succession within this very large operation, I saw first-hand how an

organization took succession extremely seriously. I relocated several times for this company and continued my journey of developing my professional skills as a human resource professional. As a result, I took a job with a family-owned health network. After watching some family dynamics, it increased my awareness and fueled my fascination even more regarding succession. I left the health network company and secured a job with a very large Fortune 25 manufacturing company, United Technologies Sikorsky Aircraft. I ran HR for three of its subsidiaries, which were at one time family-owned businesses. With this experience, I then took a job with a family-owned generic pharmaceutical company. It was this company and the family dynamics there that inspired the decision to earn my PhD and study family dynamics in succession planning. In this job, I was required to travel to China several times a year, and in one of my travels, I met a gentleman who earned his PhD later in life. To say I was captivated is an understatement. He would be out in the field training and teaching and then go back to the classroom to impart his experiences. Right away, I knew I had to do this. I knew it wouldn't be easy though. How would I fit this into my life as an executive leader of HR, adjunct professor at The University of New Haven, husband, and father to two young girls, as well as deal with the typical mid-life issues that we all face? I knew I had to be true to my personal ambitions of continuous learning, and I also knew I had to set an example for my daughters. I had to pass down this work ethic, this contagious and endless energy, and show them hard work and rewards require sacrifices. Weren't these the same lessons passed down to me?

I could not get this out of my head. I found myself in the evenings researching various PhD programs and different versions of succession planning. I knew at that moment I needed to take the journey and return to school and study succession planning in family businesses. I am thrilled to share in this book some highlights of my research study and some of the findings that helped me create an assessment to help business owners, family business advisors, lawyers, CPAs, human resource professionals, as well as countless others who work within family businesses. Each chapter of this book will target the categories that were developed from that research.

Your Time to Reflect:

- *Is there still a "journey" in you?*
- *Do you have a plan in place to get there? Do you have a team of support?*
- *What excites you? What frightens you?*

CHAPTER 2

HISTORY OF SUCCESSION PLANNING

For this chapter, the professor in me needs to teach right now and turn to the past to help you understand the present and the future. That is the reason the history of succession planning is found at the onset of this book. I admit that as I was researching the history of succession planning, I was peeling away at my own curiosity of this topic. Why wasn't the history of succession planning addressed in the past? How many different succession processes are there? Was I missing something?

With the history of succession and the different ways to think and plan for succession, it will be important for family owners to customize a process and system that works for them. It should not be just about finding a replacement but honoring the past, celebrating the present, and planning for the future when it comes to ensuring that the traditions and norms are passed down from generation to generation.

A variety of elements are included in a succession planning transition, but the primary purpose of such planning is to identify the pool of potential successors (Christension, 1953). In the early studies of the 1950s, researchers concentrated on executive development plans, performance appraisals, the establishment of replacement tables, and the development of high potential candidates. From 1980 on, succession planning research received greater attention than in previous years (Kesner & Sebora, 1994). The main finding from a historical perspective is that a process and system need to be followed to help influence the success of succession planning transitions within a business (Mehrabani & Mohamad, 2011).

What stands out to me, historically, is that between 1950 through 2009, FOBs and organizations focused on replacing key positions and concentrated on their future paths. What these studies neglect is that to push forward, business owners need to secure what they have learned from their past and assess how they are doing in their current state. Past research in succession planning was conducted to look at ways to strengthen the pool of candidates (Walker, 1998). A summary of key studies in succession planning from 1950 through 2009 is presented in Table 1. FOB owners need to be cognizant of the following to help prepare themselves for a successful succession transition.

Table 1

Historical Succession Planning from 1950 Through 2009

Year	Key Studies	Key Researchers	Key Findings
1950 - 1959	A few empirical studies were conducted regarding management and CEO development rather than true succession planning.	Chapman – 1954	Studies helped identify characteristics of candidates to be considered for development into critical positions.
1960 - 1969	Grosky (1960) forwarded the vicious-cycle theory that described how succession planning brought about trouble and chaos through changes in policies and procedures.	Grosky – 1960 Throw – 1961	There was a strong connection between planning for succession and profitability of a business.

1970 - 1979	Research showed manpower and action-planning to look at in-house capabilities.	Colman – 1970	It was important to develop objectives and goals of succession planning. Development of staffing needs was a result of planning for succession transition.
1980 - 1989	Several studies regarding succession planning and replacement planning programs were completed. Comparison study was on general succession planning and CEO succession. 60 companies had CEOs who passed away suddenly.	Carnazza – 1982 Mahler – 1983 Rhodes & Walker – 1984 Friedman – 1984 Hall – 1986 Warrell & Davidson – 1987	It was important to ensure the development of an adequate number of qualified workforces in key professional and managerial positions that may become vacant in the future. Businesses would have operated better if successors were named immediately.
1990-1999	HR executives were from 1,968 publicly traded firms. A prolonged study was conducted with 94 publicly held companies in the US, starting in 1992-1998	Huselid – 1995 Ciampa & Watkins– 1999	High performance work practices were associated with employee engagement, retention, and organizational performance. 5 years later, only 25% of candidates brought in from the outside were promoted into key positions

| 2000 – 2009 | Several studies focused on succession planning and how they fit with their individual businesses. In the 2000s, researchers started to expand to other business organizations such as family-owned, healthcare, and Educational establishments.

Quantitative studies were conducted with 604 family-owned Canadian businesses. | Baruch & Peiperl– 2000

Sharma, Chrisman, & Chua – 2003 | Succession management was an important attribute of effective career management.

There was not a "one size fits all" plan.

Owners should have filled the pipeline with high performing people to ensure that every leadership level had an abundance of its performers from which to draw. Succession planning improved satisfaction. |

Succession planning is not an easy process for any business if it does not have a systematic method in place. FOBs bring a unique set of issues besides running the business and selecting the right successors for the next generation; they also need to think about how the succession planning transition impacts the family (Wee & Ibrahim, 2012). CEOs or owners of FOBs may struggle to find the right sibling, child, or relative who has the skills, knowledge, and ability to run the business. They may also feel a sense of obligation to pass the business to their children and may not be able to think of the additional workforce that a different type of business may have.

Succession planning within FOBs is comprised of an array of components, all focused on matching leaders and future leaders to key organizational positions which require special knowledge, skills, and experiences. Researchers suggest that there are four major components in the succession planning transition for FOBs: the trigger phase, the preparation phase, the selection phase, and the training phase (Breton-Miller et al., 2004; Brockhaus, 2004; Chrisman & Chua; DeMassis, 2008; Murray, 2003). The first component, the trigger phase, occurs when the family-owner has thought of his exit strategy and is ready and willing to hand over his business to someone in his family or to a

7

nonfamily member (Murray, 2003). The owner needs to communicate effectively with all the right people within the business and in his family on the specific timeline of the exit strategy.

The second phase of succession planning is the preparation component, in which the owner develops a vision of how the business should function in the future, including identifying goals, ground rules, and clear expectations for all who are involved in the succession planning transition (Breton-Miller et al., 2004). This phase includes a possibly new organizational structure to help identify the resources the company needs to function with the employees no longer in their critical roles.

The third phase of the process is selection, or setting the criteria for the possible candidates who could take over for the owner or incumbent (Michel & Kammerlander, 2014). This is important so that the incumbent feels satisfied when the successor has the proper leadership skills to secure the business. Satisfaction occurs when the incumbent has the confidence of possessing the skills, knowledge, and ability to lead the business in developing its revenue, operate it with efficiency, and have a plan to develop both the family and nonfamily employees.

The fourth and final stage of the succession process is the training of the successor and developing the relationships between the incumbent and the internal and external stakeholders who would be impacted by the transfer of power and ownership (Brockhaus, 2004). Once this stage has been agreed upon between the successor and incumbent, a communication plan needs to be developed. This plan addresses who the communication is for, what it will entail, and its timeline with each of the stakeholders. The message may be developed and delivered in different formats, such as written communication via emails and letters, and in personal meetings, such as executive board meetings, department staff meetings, and external customer visits.

The process of effective succession planning for all businesses is outlined by Rothwell (2010) as a seven-step process (see Table 2). Each of these seven steps represents a key part of the succession process, allowing for effective and efficient transition of power within a business.

When businesses follow the seven steps, they are more likely to commit to a successful transition process.

Table 2

Seven-Step Succession Process Performance

Phase	Steps	Key Points
Trigger	1st	Identify long-term vision and direction
Preparation	2nd	Assess status of productivity and talent requirements
Preparation	3rd	Evaluate employee performance and identify talent
Preparation	4th	Evaluate future work by identifying recruitment and retention strategies
Selection	5th	Identify and develop high potential employees within the business
Training of the Successor	6th	Develop a plan to close gaps on any developmental needs
Training of the Successor	7th	Develop an evaluation and tracking process

During the first step, the leadership makes a commitment toward a succession plan. This means that to begin the process of succession planning transition, the leadership must identify the long-term vision and direction of the business (Epstein, 2010). This process is accomplished by looking at the strengths, weaknesses, opportunities, and threats to the business.

In the second step, the leadership needs to assess the status of productivity and the talent requirements needed to continue to function optimally long term. By reviewing the weaknesses of the current staff, the leadership identifies what is needed to fill the gaps. When leaders address the gaps regarding talent, they can focus on placing the talent in the needed areas (Rothwell, 2010).

Throughout the third step, the business evaluates employee performance, identifying talent by using critical assessment tools to rate employees' competencies (Byham, 2002). This process allows for the identification of a pool of qualified candidates and their developmental needs. By developing the needs of the qualified employees, the leadership has a choice in regard to selecting the right person for the right position within the business.

In the fourth step, businesses evaluate future work and talent requirements by identifying both recruitment and retention strategies to attract, develop, and retain talent (Rothwell, Jackson, Ressler, Jones, & Brower, 2015). In this step, the leaders review current job descriptions to make sure the proper skills, knowledge, and ability are stated to attract the right talent for the business. By developing the job descriptions, the business can attract new employees who fully understand what is expected of them and who are fully capable of filling critical positions.

In the fifth step, the business identifies and develops high potential employees within the business for upward mobility. Once these high-potential employees are identified, the business develops and implements learning opportunities, both formal and informal, to monitor progress of the high potentials and be able to provide the proper opportunities for them to grow and develop (Baron & Armstrong, 2008). By providing high potential employees opportunities to stretch themselves with assignments, they learn critical skills needed to progress to higher level positions.

In the sixth step, businesses develop a plan to close the gaps on any developmental needs. This is accomplished through the design of a performance management process that provides continuous communication about the employees' performances and commitments to their own development and growth. By providing feedback for both improvement and recognition, leaders help their employees' developmental needs and strengthen core areas of their performance (Epstein, 2010).

Finally, the seventh step directs the FOB to develop an evaluation procedure to continuously improve on the succession planning transition.

For this final step, the FOB develops a tracking process to record the development of the high potential candidates by analyzing feedback from all the different stakeholders, both internally and externally (Rothwell, 2010). When the business provides constructive feedback from all the stakeholders, this strengthens the succession planning transition by allowing its employees to develop and grow.

According to Shirley (2008), a five-step succession plan model identifies the need for senior organizational commitment and vision based on the business' strategic goals. This model stresses the importance of talent management and designates roles within a business. This model also describes the important steps needed to recognize such talent within a business and identify the recruitment and retention of a successor (see Table 3).

Table 3
Organizational Commitment and Vision through the Five-Step Succession Plan Model (Shirley, 2008)

Identify both where and who is ready and what areas of skills need to be developed.

Identify an individual for a targeted role.

Involve the development of a role and assign mentor and coaching opportunities.

Evaluate the employee selected for the succession.

Develop both recruitment and retention strategies to help keep the identified successor.

Many family business advisors agree that succession planning transitions in their businesses are limited in their effectiveness (Church, 2014). Succession planning is often regarded as another complex and time-consuming human resource process, or paper exercise to be completed and archived until the next year's review (Huselid, 1995). As shown in Table 4, there are nine observations that address the limited effectiveness of succession planning.

Table 4

Nine Observations about State of Succession Planning

Observation	Explanation
We are in love with bright and shiny objects.	Individuals tend to gravitate to people, objectives, and ideas that excited them.
We all suffer from "good driver" syndrome.	Most individuals suffer from basic attribution error, attributing higher levels of skills to themselves than to the average person on a variety of tasks.
Some senior executives care less about succession planning than others.	Some CEOs spend quality time on succession planning, and others are less interested in the concept. This may be due to other pressing concerns that are happening in real time.
We often find ourselves influencing where we could versus where we should.	Only a small number of practitioners say they could consistently set up talent agenda in a holistic way or influence the top of the business.
We have mastered the art of creating lists and checks, but to what end?	When attending any succession planning workshops, people make charts, lists, and presentations.
We often get trapped in short-term replacement planning versus long-term succession.	Many succession plans are short-term and used to fill emergency replacements.
There is no "silver bullet" for any succession plan.	People tend to look to one special tool, measurement, definition, chart, and program.

We know a great deal about talent development and succession planning.	As the topic of succession planning is being reviewed, individuals start to have plenty of data from which they could pull.
Succession planning is all about execution.	Once an individual has come up with a plan, it should be written down, and action steps should be developed to work towards it.

According to Church (2014), there are four pillars of succession planning execution. The main purpose of the pillars is to maximize the approach to ensure consistency and accountability regarding succession planning. Church expands the previously outlined observations of succession planning by introducing the four pillars of execution. See Table 5

Table 5

Four Pillars of Succession Planning Execution

Focus	Consistency	Integration	Accountability
Targets a few key areas for maximum effort and impact	Maintains a common language and approach for talent interventions	Builds a link to other subsystems and technology	Installs methods of rewards for driving quality planning and outcomes

According to my mentor, Lisë Stewart, succession planning is a vital part of ensuring the ongoing success and sustainability of the FOB and is often misunderstood (2015). Many business advisors mistakenly proclaim to "practice" succession planning with their clients because they are experienced in finding buyers. However, there are many steps involved in a development and transition plan, from setting up support systems to identifying competencies and assessing employees, to monitoring documentation and revising, when necessary, as presented in Table 6.

Table 6

Succession Plan Development and Transition

Process	Steps	Purpose	Outcomes
Set Up Succession Planning Support Systems	Identify necessary resources to complete the process (internal and external)	Ensure succession plans are articulated and necessary resources are available	A thoughtful and smooth succession process is defined.
Determine Key Position(s)	Consider how many positions require succession attention	Determine areas that might have been impacted by the transition/exit strategy	A clear map of critical roles and areas where the business could be vulnerable or enhanced is presented.
Identify Competencies	Identify the key skills, knowledge, and abilities critical for each targeted position in the company	Gain an understanding of the skill and talent pool needed at both leadership and functional levels	An understanding of what the business needs to be successful is indicated, and what a successful exit/transition looks like is also specified.
Identify & Assess Candidates	Determine which people are the best fits and where there are talent gaps	Thoughtfully fill positions with the best possible candidates	There is careful consideration and selection of the best candidates from among existing or newly recruited employees.

Create and Implement Development Plans	Identify a systematic approach to develop selected successor/ employees	Confirm the candidates have the best opportunity to be prepared for their positions	A clearly defined personal plan that is shared with successors is designated.
Measure, Monitor, and Revise	Develop documentation to track goals, analyze progress, and take corrective steps as needed	Safeguard that regular evaluations occur to help ensure successful development	The shortest time possible to prepare successful candidates is allotted.

After reviewing many different models of succession planning and transitions, I can confidently say there is not a precise model to address all the diverse aspects of a family-owned business. Each family-owned business has its own, unique set of challenges, and by exploring these obstacles, business owners can choose the proper models and transition processes that work for them. It should not be just about finding a replacement but rather a successor who believes in honoring the past, celebrating the present, and planning for the future when it comes to ensuring that the traditions and norms are passed down from generation to generation. By developing a new assessment based upon my qualitative study, I am proud to introduce another way that family-owned business owners can create their own processes, thus enhancing already existing knowledge and research, while providing new options that meet the FOB's specific needs.

Your Time to Reflect:

- *In what areas have you turned to the past to embrace your present and prepare for your future?*
- *Identify your unique set of challenges and rank them in order of importance.*
- *When you think of the word, succession, what comes to mind?*

CHAPTER 3

MY RESEARCH STUDY

Kitchen table research lab

As a Human Resource professional, or as I also like to refer to it as a Human Capital professional, I always stress the importance of deepening the bench and getting the next generation ready for leadership positions. I also find myself advising business owners and family leadership about the importance of investing in both family members and nonfamily members working in the business. I was taught early on through my training program at Stop & Shop, an original FOB that knew how to utilize this way of thinking, that it was critical for a leader to always be grooming someone for his/her position. This is a natural and informal way of having an emergency succession preparation plan in place. When I was an executive running HR for a family business, I had several conversations with the owner about his succession plan. I learned quickly that he was extremely uncomfortable discussing his plan, and I was both curious and perplexed. At this time, I also saw a few executives leave the organization, both voluntarily and involuntarily, and I wanted to better understand how succession planning impacted organizational health and employee engagement within a family-owned business.

Succession planning is a vital process for family-owned businesses and is used to describe a wide variety of activities, including identifying talent and skill gap analysis. It is really finding the right employees who can take over the business when the time comes. According to Stewart (2015), a succession planning transition consists of an exit strategy, the development of family governance, growth and value enhancement, an execution and accountability plan, leadership development and finally, the succession plan itself. One of the outcomes of my qualitative study was to explore practices that CEOs or owners in FOBs used in their succession planning transition.

My qualitative study concerns FOBs and the challenges of not having a succession planning transition in place. The estimated lifespan of an FOB is 24 years, with only 1 in 3 family businesses succeeding to the second generation (Aloulou, 2018; deVires, 1993), 1 in 8 FOBs lasting into the third generation (Blocknick, 1984; Leib & Zehrer, 2018), and even lower to 1 in 33 in the fourth generation ("Family Owned Statistics", 2016). These statistics for long-term survival rates are astounding. As I read these numbers, I immediately saw how this related directly to my father's story of owning MiKERZ pharmacy. His business lasted about 2.5 decades. I know first-hand that owners need to identify the person with the right set of skills and values who could take over the business, which is a struggle for many FOBs (deVires, 1993).

Succession planning is essential to the long-term survival of FOBs, as 40% of family business owners expect to retire within the next decade, and nearly 10.4 trillion dollars of family business owner worth will be transferred within the next two decades (Walsh, 2010). There are numerous decisions that need to be made, and much preparation needs to be done before passing the business to the next generation. It is important that owners of FOBs protect their hard work, reputation, and wealth that they have generated for their families, and when they develop a well-thought-out succession plan, they can accomplish this task. Furthermore, 35% of Fortune 500 businesses are family-controlled, which, once again, supports the need for a solid succession planning transition ("Business in the Blood", 2014). According to the U.S. Small Business Administration, 90% of all businesses in the U.S. are family-owned and need to address the topic of succession planning transition (Walsh, 2010).

The purpose of my qualitative study was to explore practices that CEOs or owners in FOBs used in their succession planning transition to maintain the overall organizational health of the business and to better understand their perception of employee engagement. There were three research questions that drove my study: 1. What were the practices that CEOs or owners in FOBs used in their succession planning transition? 2. How did the CEO or owner's perception of organizational health impact the likelihood of a succession planning transition? 3. How did the CEO or owner's perception of employee engagement impact the succession planning transition?

One of the outcomes of my qualitative research study was to explore practices that CEOs or owners of FOBs used in their succession planning transition. Through the lens of organizational health, employee engagement, and succession planning transition, I can now better understand the CEO or owner's perception that impacts the outcome of these three conceptual frameworks (see Figure 1). These three conceptual frameworks were instrumental as I developed semi-structured interview questions for my participants, and these three conceptual frameworks will be discussed in detail in future chapters as I break down the assessment by categories.

Figure 1. Conceptual framework.

After conducting historical research and reading numerous articles, I was not seeing solid information regarding second generation succession planning that tried to increase those percentages from one generation to the next. I was still wrestling to uncover the lessons from one generation to the next, and I wanted to get this conversation explored. Not finding significant data on this topic drove my desire to analyze and understand the lived experiences even more. As I thought about my father's business and how I would have been a second-generation owner, I was trying to put myself in the shoes of those owners who contemplate the difficult decision of keeping the business or selling it.

By exploring succession planning in FOBs, I developed a new assessment to help CEOs or owners prepare for their future transitions. Interviewing CEOs or owners of FOBs helped me identify how they viewed succession planning transitions in relationship to the organizational health of the business and employee engagement. Gaining a better understanding and determining if it mattered to owners how employees felt if there was a clear path to succession reinforced the significance of succession planning in the future. Electing not to interview employees for this study demonstrates the importance of the

CEO or owner's perception and perspective because succession planning starts at the leadership level.

Based on research looking at 20 different qualitative research studies from 2000 to 2018, I followed this approach and interviewed 15 owners who experienced a succession planning transition to help develop practices of succession planning. The sample size ranged from 3 to 25 owners, and each interview lasted approximately 1.5 hours. The businesses represented a diverse group of industries, including size in both revenue and headcount, as well as locations throughout the United States.

In thinking about who would be included in the research study, I established the following participant criteria:

- Must have been the CEO or owner of the FOB.
- Must have experienced a Succession Plan Transition.
- There must have been at least two other family members working in the FOB.
- The business must have been in operation for more than 20 years.
- The business must have had at least 20 employees.
- The business could have been from any industry.
- The business must have been in the United States.

I analyzed the data collected through semi-structured interviews using Interpretative Phenomenological Analysis (IPA), a qualitative research approach committed to the examination of how people made sense of their major life experiences (Smith et al., 2013). The questions for the semi-structured interview contained three parts. The first part of the questioning targeted demographic questions. By starting with these types of questions, I wanted to put the interviewees at ease, but I also wanted to obtain critical information about the business's size, location, years in operation, and so forth. The second part of the questioning explored the practices of the succession planning transition. The third part of the questioning focused on the owners' perceptions of employee engagement regarding the succession planning transition. All questions were reviewed by Lisë Stewart, founder and Principal-in-Charge of Eisner Amper's Center for Family Business Excellence.

Both practical and theoretical significance were important for me when I was developing my research criteria and the questions I wanted answered. I wanted to develop a useful tool and provide scholarly information that could be used for future studies. Researchers have long stressed the importance of succession planning to ensure the continuity and prosperity of a business. Some researchers have even extended this concept by asserting succession planning was the primary contribution that one generation could bestow upon the next and must have been managed as such (Ayres, 1990). The practical significance of my qualitative study can help both the organizational development and human resource practitioners better understand how the owners in the businesses perceive their organizational health and employee engagement regarding their succession planning transitions. The outcomes of the study developed the assessment that can then be used to help CEOs, owners, and practitioners develop the proper tools and methodologies of the succession planning transition process. I targeted the individuals who would care about the research findings, including the CEOs or owners of the FOBs, the possible family and nonfamily successors, the family members who were not directly involved in the business but had a financial interest with the business, as well as external stakeholders who are directly and indirectly impacted by the succession of the family business and economic outlook.

Theoretical significance relates to the impact on future theories regarding organizational health, employee engagement, and the succession planning transition. Regarding my qualitative study, the theoretical significance demonstrated that the succession planning transitions in businesses were limited in their effectiveness. By examining the perceptions of CEOs or owners through the lens of organizational health, employee engagement, and succession planning transitions, the practices helped develop future research to address how such perceptions played a part in how CEOs or owners viewed the succession planning transition.

I learned that CEOs or owners of FOBs needed to gain a better understanding of the succession planning transition and the impact that it had on the organizational health of the business and employee engagement. In the next decade, there will be a tremendous amount of wealth and resources transitioned to the next generations, and CEOs or owners will need to utilize succession planning transitions to stay engaged and to keep their businesses competitive in the market.

One of the primary outcomes of this qualitative study was the development of an assessment to assist practitioners, scholars, and other CEOs or owners with identifying the level of preparedness for succession planning processes. Another significant finding was that the CEOs or owners needed to be respectful of their past and mindful of the present to be prepared for the future. As I reflect on this journey to better understand the CEOs' or owners' perceptions and practices of how they perceive employee engagement and the organizational health of the succession planning transition, I learned that one size does not fit all, and utilizing an assessment can help formulate a plan that targets the needs of each unique family-owned business. In the next several chapters, you will see some of my research unfold. The categories of the assessment are a direct result of my interviews and the data collection from the 15 CEO/owners interviewed.

Phenomenological research is a systematic process that helps identify themes and reflections based upon the lived everyday experiences of the participants (Husserl, 1927). For IPA research to be successful, I made interpretations based on reading within the terms of the text which had been provided by the participants. Based on their answers to the semi-structured interview questions, I was able to interpret their meanings and categorize them. Another key theoretical part of IPA came from hermeneutics, the theory of interpretation (Smith et al., 2013). IPA methodology operates with what is known as double hermeneutics, as I was trying to make sense of the participants while trying to make sense of the world (Smith & Osborn, 2015). For example, when I interviewed one business owner, I would interpret that lived experience, which increased my knowledge after interviewing others who shared similar experiences.

I learned while doing my research that qualitative researchers rarely work with a fixed body of data (Richards, 1999). Data that is collected comes in quite different forms, such as observations, interviews, and document analysis. MaxQDA is a qualitative, data analysis software that offers a range of resources to help research and recognize themes and categories. This software helped me code and analyze qualitative data from interviews, focus groups, and online surveys and was a tool for recording and linking ideas and exploring patterns (Maietta et al., 2007). I worked with one of my mentor professors in the program to teach me the MaxQDA tool and how to use IPA properly. This process took a good 6 months of weekly lab work but was well worth every moment I spent in and outside the lab.

Using MaxQDA, I then defined clusters to help identify similar data to develop a theme. Clusters was a theory process that was identified as a method of empirical, phenomenological analysis (Bazeley, 2009). The cluster process helped enable the data collection, helped with conceptual clarity through the coding process, and helped with the identification of patterns. By identifying clusters and themes through proper coding, I developed a succession planning transition model from the practices identified by the participants.

Your Time to Reflect:

- *Were any questions you may have had answered in this chapter?*
- *Do you have more written down that you hope will be answered in the following chapters?*
- *What research have you done in this area?*
- *Why do you believe succession planning and succession planning transition are keys to your business?*

CHAPTER 4

SUCCESSION TRANSITION
ASSESSMENT MEASUREMENT
FOR PREPARATION:
PURPOSE, PROCESS,
APPROACH & OBJECTIVES
OF THE ASSESSMENT

The purpose of The Kerzner STAMP is to help CEO/business owners understand how prepared they are for a succession planning transition, both formally and informally. The Kerzner STAMP develops a more formal transition plan by addressing any gaps that have been identified. It also helps owners look at what they have done in the past and are doing in the present, so that they can then best plan for the future.

There are four steps in this assessment process:

- Step One: Answer the questions in the assessment
- Step Two: Think through the scoring and assign a score for each item
- Step Three: Develop an action plan or list of any items that score 1.5 or higher

- Step Four: Develop a project plan with deliverables from each category that need to be addressed regarding the gaps identified

As CEOs/owners of FOBs or Family Advisors read through the assessment, they need to make sure there is a clear understanding of what each category means and how it is relevant and defined for their own businesses. These leaders need to then work with other family members or Family Business Advisors, so it is not completed by just them alone. Having a systematic approach will help alleviate some of the emotional rollercoasting family business owners experience juggling the family needs, the business needs, as well as their ownership needs in the next phase of their lives.

It is crucial for CEOs and owners to determine how prepared they are for a future succession planning transition. This assessment will identify any gaps in the planning process and target creative ways to honor past successes, while embracing the future. Developing a more formal succession plan reduces the resistance or the conflict that the business owner may feel by having some control over his or her destiny. In my opinion, being able to transition with dignity is the ultimate goal.

Your Time to Reflect:

- *What's your initial impression of STAMP? What questions do you have?*
- *How would you use STAMP in your succession planning?*
- *What do you want protected from your past? What's sacred in your present? What does your future look like personally and professionally?*
- *Can you transition with dignity?*

CHAPTER 5

FAMILY HISTORY

As we get into this chapter, you will hear from many of the participants throughout my research study, and their stories and affirmations solidify my assumptions. However, I wanted to share a little of my own family history with you first in this chapter. Succession for my father was something he did not have to wrestle with because he knew early on that his children would not go into the profession. Yet, succession in my family was also not about wealth transfer or about owning a family business. In my family, it was more about the lessons concerning business, personal integrity, and passing down traditions that sustain our family legacy. For example, we pass down family traditions, such as special practices of blessings at all the revered moments in life. We cherish a bottle of Crown Royale that is purchased at the beginning of one's life or special moments. That bottle will stay with the individual or couple and will be used at those special occasions, including baby naming, bris, bar or bat mitzvah, high school and college graduation, as well as any other personal and professional achievements. At family blessings, we welcome and honor our past, represent our present, and have this bottle with us in the future.

Father toasting the next generation

It was important for me to have a better understanding of what family meant and be able to relate to any of the information that was being provided to me by my research participants. So, in saying that, it is first important to define families. Families are defined as people who have shared history, experiences, emotional connections, and a set of common goals. Defining what constitutes a family-owned business I found was not that clear cut, as there was not a "typical" FOB, and not all families adhered to the nuclear structure, with families having many varied components (Carsud, Perez, & Sachs, 1996). In my deep dive into the research, I found that the divorce rate in the United States was 50% for first marriages, 67% for second marriages, and 73% for third marriages (Banschick, 2010; Mathis, 2017). There are currently 1.4 million family-owned businesses "jointly" owned and equally operated by a husband and wife (Anderson & Anderson, 2018). With the current statistics for divorce rates at a high level, it is important that couples who worked together have a succession planning transition in place and understand how the business would operate if the marriage dissolved. Additionally, families evolve with every new marriage or marriage that generates a new birth or attends to a death; thus, any definition of family encompasses these dynamic aspects.

Owner-specific challenges in family-owned businesses present unique dilemmas and frustrations for owners and those who work for them (Kepner, 1983). Leading and managing FOBs is a calling, more than a job, because running this type of business has profound meaning and importance for owners; this establishes a unique set of challenges because the bond with the company may have greater meaning than the monetary rewards the owners obtain from owning and running the business (Caspersz & Thomas, 2015). Because of this calling to run an FOB, it is difficult for the CEO or owner and the family to unleash control and pass it on to a successor. Due to this bond, FOBs are considered emotional arenas more so than nonfamily businesses. Emotions could run exceedingly high with family members who work for FOBs, and this could cause the risk of emotional distress, emotional burnout (Grandey, 2000; Härtel & Hsu, 2002), and physical illness (Schaubroeck & Jones, 2000).

Family members who are involved with the day-to-day operations and those who are owners who have a financial stake may not agree with the direction of the business, which could cause a stressful situation. Family relationships are considered strong during challenging times, but relationships among families' members could cause business conflicts and powerplays among relatives; the issues not only split up families, but also cause the business to fail (Fineman, 2000). Thus, understanding emotions and how they impact the family in FOBs is important because it establishes an emotional climate and determines how employees view the business (Ashkanasy, 2003).

As an owner of a family business, there can be signs and symptoms of owner resistance. Owners of FOBs need to not only deal with being a business owner, but they need to also manage being a leader of the family. Because of this, they may become frightened of losing their identity within the family structure that they have created (Lansberg, 1983). Succession planning transition is a topic that faces resistance from business owners because of the changes in relationships within the family throughout the transition (Lansberg, 1988). Some of the changes that occur target the family system, including the role of the family members and their independence on the subsystems of the FOB and the owner (Sharma, Chrisman, & Chua, 1997).

Another change could be understood through the organizational development and the influence of time in the business regarding the relationship of the owner's disengagement with the growth of the business. Owners of FOBs struggle with how to separate their responsibilities as the head of the house and the owner of the business. One question that researchers try to answer regarding succession planning within FOBs is, "Is it family first or business first?" Researchers state that a current issue and challenge for FOB leaders is managing family relationships, and this could impact balancing the different interests that the owner has such as his family life and his professional life in the business (Family Business Institute, 2016; Getz & Carlsen, 2000).

Resistance to succession planning in FOBs also stems from psychological and emotional issues that surface with the owners because of the bond they create with the company; these issues interfere or delay the succession planning transition (Handler & Kram, 1988). There are several themes in research that link the owner's childhood experiences, such as living in poverty, not wanting to feel insecure, and experiencing the sudden death of a parent, to the drive of an individual to want to be his own person and run an operation that he could control (Collins, Moore, & Unwalla, 1964). The psychological memories of the past could also drive a person to start a business, so he would naturally resist any change that interferes with the safety of that operation and the family members who are part of that business. As a result, leaders often do not want to give up their influence or power, both before and even after the transition of responsibility has taken place (Marler et al., 2017).

Owners of FOBs view their business as an extension of themselves and giving it up to others is like giving up a piece of themselves (Handler, 1990; Ket de Vries, 1985). Another psychological element is the fear of aging or dying. Without question, succession planning is something owners do not want to think about when they are still active and healthy (Lansberg, 1988).

Succession between generations is not an economic act of transferring wealth, but rather a meaningful investment with social history, values, and culture (Hjorth & Dawson, 2016). Family members who work for FOBs often share an emotional bond in addition to the bloodline they share with others within the business (Chua, 1999; Stewart, 2015). Family members of an FOB also share history and accumulate experiences, but they interpret them very differently, which could impact their view of other family members and the business itself (Gersick, Davis, Hampton, & Lansberg, 1997).

Understanding family history provides future direction for the FOB and describes how the CEO or owner views the succession planning transition from distinct levels of the business. When the CEO or owner thinks strategically about his exit strategy for retirement or contemplates options to sell the FOB, there are some areas that need to be addressed to ensure a successful succession planning transition. Understanding family history includes considering the external influences of the succession planning transition process, as well as the internal influences of providing early communication to all employees and family members on the timing and process of the succession planning transition.

Individuals experience life events of varying degrees, such as unexpected illness, divorce, and the death of a family member; however, when this occurred for some of the participants in my study, the impact extended to their businesses, not just their personal lives. Understanding FOB history and understanding past generations helps employees understand why being an FOB is important to the CEOs or owners. Many participants noted that having visuals displaying important reminders about the foundation of the workforce and the principles upon which the company was built in the board rooms, conference rooms, and breakrooms strengthened the understanding of their family history.

In honoring past generations, participants admired and valued the origins of their businesses and the traditions upon which they were based. Various participants communicated that when their employees learned about the past CEOs or owners and the traditions that made the business what it was, they understood the importance of family history. One participant shared, "We do a little of the Chinese ancestor worship. The photographs of our founders are prominently displayed in the board room. The research facilities are named after the founders, cofounders." Another participant shared his system for honoring past generations.

> We do pretty simple things like we have a four pillars award. The pillars are driven from the personalities of the four siblings that built the business as well as the ones passed down from the founders of culture because a lot of businesses, if they're family-based, the evolution of the culture is started from the first generation, my parents. But then, having the four pillars from the analysis of the four leaders, we provide awards, a little recognition awards and a little bump in the paycheck for people that exemplify those pillars that drive engagement.

Some participants communicated that using family photographs of the founding owners educated both family members and nonfamily members about the history and sacrifices that cultivated and advanced the FOB. Another participant revealed, "Photographs of our founders are prominently displayed. We never miss the opportunity to mention that. What else does family mean? Yeah. It means you protect your people." While protecting and embracing one's family history, the current ownership ensures a successful planning transition.

Learning about past successors and the origins of their businesses, many participants stated that the relationships between the CEO or owner and their children impacted the succession planning transition regarding who obtained the power to run, own, and lead the FOB. Those participants agreed that having a specific transition plan was critical in helping prevent future conflicts. When thinking about sibling relationships and the future direction and ownership of the FOB, many participants considered the following questions:

- Who would run the operations of the FOB, and who would be the CEO?
- Would all siblings get ownership opportunities?
- How would they divide the parents' estate so there would be equity?
- How would the siblings resolve conflicts that might arise in the future?

One participant allowed his future generation a voice in the direction of the FOB and stated:

> In 1984, my father wanted to retire at age 50, so he did a quick exit, which has been proven by research to be a strong predicator of successful transitions. He pretty much let the sibling team take it where they wanted to take it with his exit.

Thinking about one's own transition can be emotionally taxing for a CEO or owner, but multiple participants commented that exiting the business with enough time to think through the process helped drive the plan for the next generation. One of the participants offered that once his plan was written down, the roadmap was then communicated to the family.

> My relationship is very good with my dad, and we started having a conversation about his vision of the company and my involvement. At the time of our conversation, we started to get a better understanding of who we are and how we view things currently and in the future of the FOB. Once my dad saw that I had a big interest in getting more involved and wanting to take over, he tasked me in getting all the information we needed for the succession planning process. I found the right attorneys, estate attorneys, accountants. Soon after that first meeting, we started to transfer some stock.

Another participant shared that starting early and utilizing the proper resources made it less likely to make hasty decisions, redo, stall, or display resistance to the transition process and commented:

> Maybe it's time to start thinking about this. So, I initiated conversations with an estate attorney that I trusted and to have my best interest, and I thought this person was good, fair, and came from a very good law firm. That estate attorney started working with my father and his existing CPA and discussions were made, and I think the first round of gifting was done in that manner.

In understanding family history, some participants stated that when founding generations did not require all children to work in the family business, this developed a culture where family members could have a choice to enter or not into the FOB. If there was not a family member willing, or able, to take over the business, one of the participants commented that he needed to think about selling the business and ensure the business was, in fact, marketable to sell.

> I remember over the years, my father, when I was in my 30s, we talked about a business being sold and he would say things like, "There's probably no family member that wants to pick business and a gift or buy the stock of family members to perpetuate the business." It's been a kind of a sad conversation about them, and I'm hoping that my daughter and any other cousins that might get involved will add value to the treasure of that family business.

Numerous participants articulated that FOBs with multigenerational leadership greatly benefitted from the countless lessons learned from understanding the family history and discovering the methods leaders utilized to handle the succession planning process. One participant proudly stated, "My great, great grandfather started it with his son together." Another responded, "As CEO, I respect what my father has built and because of this, I think this is why we do not have any major emotional issues regarding the business." And, yet another participant added, "So he and I can relate well, it's rare we get into an emotional issue. It's for the most part we're on the same page. I respect his position and what he's built." Understanding, respect, and tradition are key terms that those participants relayed when learning from the past.

Both family and nonfamily members who work in the FOB assume different responsibilities. Some stated that family members should be cross-trained to provide backup or support to other family members. One participant supported this by saying, "I am president, CEO. I've been involved since 1985 when my grandpa was diagnosed. I became president in 2008 and CEO I guess shortly thereafter. It was almost like a dual role." The participants and family employees who accepted different roles and worked in different departments added value to the business as they stepped in and provided consistency throughout the stages of the transition.

FOBs are made of family members, both of blood and by marriage. Each member plays a vital role within the business, keeping the family's legacy alive and driving the mission, vision, and values of the FOB. One CEO stated that when the next generations entered the business, they preserved the lessons from the past and added to the legacy of living in the present.

> So, my father, who retired as CEO, is still chairman of the board, so he's still employed technically. I work with my two sisters; one is a marketing person, the other one is in IT, and then my husband is executive vice president at the subsidiary. So that would make, I guess including me, five in total.

Several participants noted that the children of FOBs gained opportunities other employees did not, whether it was related to salaries, bonuses, or other fringe benefits. One participant affirmed, "But if the company has a great year, I'll do an additional bonus plan for him, as my brother and as a 25-year veteran of the business, kind of a sweetener for him." Another participant added, "Some degree we were given that opportunity because we were family. In some ways, I think my brother and I got an opportunity that we probably couldn't have gotten if it weren't a family business." These participants disclosed that some of their opportunities resulted because they were family.

Participants remarked that nonfamily employees were aware that when family members joined the business, the family members were being trained to eventually take over the leadership positions. One participant stated, "It was clear to them from the beginning that I was being groomed to be the successor." However, participants also relayed that nonfamily members were a critical part of the success of the next generation, understanding the family history and learning the different roles and responsibilities of the FOB. When all employees are aware of their future assignments and expectations during a transition process, current CEOs or owners spend quality time educating the next generation about the business and how to sustain it.

Family employees may not always be qualified to perform the work they are doing; they are given opportunities because they have the DNA of the CEO or owner. Some participants remarked that family councils helped set up the rules on how family members obtained their jobs and positions. If a family member was not performing or violated the rules, the council helped the FOB manage that family member. A few participants also commented that it was beneficial for a separate group to handle the salary and benefits for family members and to safeguard this information to nonfamily employees.

Another important aspect that family owners must deal with is sibling relationships. As previously stated, multiple participants agreed clear instructions were necessary to determine who would have ownership in the future, and some participants stated that it was important to ask how did the family ensure equality among the siblings? When siblings were co-owners and played different roles within the FOB, they had a discussion of how they would communicate to the workforce and their senior leaders.

Some participants stated that a sibling code of conduct was developed to help them understand these issues and analyze areas of expertise and opportunities. One participant asserted, "Getting their technical roles covered and then planning for their exit has been my priority." Each sibling helped complement the other siblings, keeping in mind their family's history and moving the business in a forward direction.

As the FOB grows with different generations, it becomes more complex, not just in dealing with siblings, but with cousins as well. Various participants agreed that FOBs and families should develop a family council to address how cousins interacted within the FOB, how they got along, and how they resolved any conflicts that might arise. One participant stated, "I think people struggle with that from the sibling team to the cousin team because it's difficult if you've got two, three, four, five siblings working together. Exiting them without selling the family business is a big challenge." Being proactive and keeping the FOB's culture, values, and norms at the forefront of the business helps business owners minimize potential discord.

The perceptions of how employees might feel after the CEO or owner retires are also important to consider. When a CEO or owner is ready to retire and transition the FOB to the next generation, some employees are resistant to the changes because they feel that the perks and the working conditions would also change. When a new incumbent secures the leadership role, he may be more energized to move the focus to performance and grow the business. The incumbent might then want all employees to raise the bar on their current involvement in the day-to-day operations.

Many participants mentioned that because some employees felt uncomfortable, this should have been part of the strategy when developing the succession plan transition. One owner confirmed that responses from his employees concerning this would be mixed.

> I believe some individuals who like clarity on expectations and really are about more of a traditional corporate culture would welcome that kind of succession, because the indecisiveness I referenced earlier, and being

somewhat sensitive to the emotional impact of decisions, I think is a source of frustration for some, but I feel like many others would feel as if the ride is coming to an end, the gravy train is over, and now we actually have to work in a way that we didn't in the past, and that could be tough.

Multiple participants revealed that it was necessary to meet with the senior leaders of the business and obtain feedback on how their employees were feeling. The key to a successful succession transition is to make the process as seamless as possible, which means that upfront work is needed to help the employees adjust to the change.

Many participants asserted that a good process to follow when planning for the succession transition was to make the incumbent have a position like Chief Operation Officer (COO) or Vice President (VP). In that case, the other senior leaders would report to the incumbent for a period and adjust to his leadership style. One owner stated that by having a path of progression for a family member to take the helm of the FOB and socialize with the workforce, employees became accustomed to the future incumbent.

> I think the people that went through the transition with me and my dad, they were pretty much all my direct reports anyway. So, as the VP of the company, or I say, "VP role" that I held for probably four or five years prior to transition to CEO, most of the employees either worked directly for me or through a structure that was completely underneath me anyway. So, they were very comfortable when I transitioned to CEO, most of them. It was like, "Oh, no, not a whole lot's going to change." I'm in good shape.

CEOs and owners who do not have a systematic process in place relied upon their current senior leaders, without knowing if they had the knowledge, skills, and abilities to take over the FOB. One participant shared, "Currently it's an informal plan, but I'm working against a formalized plan with the support of others, both external and internal." Another business owner added that it was critical to the success of the FOB that the participants knew exactly what the employees were doing and then filled the needs of the business as they kept in mind the needs of the future.

> I would say we have an informal succession plan because there is no formal written plan for succession. It's something obviously since I'm 70 years old that I've been thinking about. But I think that, in general, I think about it not as narrowly as who will be my successor, but rather more broadly as building succession planning into the fabric of the company.

Established on the principles of growing the business, continuous improvement, and knowing which employees are in their pipeline, a formal succession plan is in the minds of many CEOs or owners, regardless of age. When CEOs or owners have an informal succession plan, they obtain feedback from friends instead of professionals such as attorneys, accountants, or other trusted advisors. However, professionals are the ones who should be held accountable and have the knowledge and skills to help a family member see future success with the FOB. Informal succession planning needs to be reworked to formal succession planning, ensuring that the FOB advances financially and all employees are aware of the steps that would be taken throughout the succession transition process.

Planning for the future varies from business to business. The timeframe for a CEO or owner starting the transition process ranges from taking over immediately because of a sudden illness, to one lasting a few years to decades. In cases when an FOB experiences a crisis, like an illness or death, numerous participants commented that it was essential to have some processes in place for succession planning or the possible selling of the FOB. One participant admitted,

We had never run a profit and loss statement, we didn't have a balance sheet complete with inventory, we didn't know the value of the real estate and so many things on it or that the company had just never done until we were obligated to do them to make a transition successful.

Another owner offered information about a five-year strategic plan and communicated, "That was the beginning. We've built our plan around a five-year plan so that my mom could retire at 65, and so we bought 49% of her shares in 2013. We bought the other 51% in 2018." Part of the timing included when and how the CEO or owner planned to retire and when the incumbent would be given full control of the FOB. Senior leaders would be interviewed, and a plan would be put in place outlining what additional skills and knowledge they would need when the new CEO or owner takes over.

When CEOs or owners in my study developed their five-year strategic plan, for many, it included people development and what and who would need to be developed to ensure the business was ready for the future. One CEO stated, "My father bought this farmland at all these different locations. The facilities were not very sophisticated, but a lot of land was there. He had the foresight to buy a lot of farmlands, and it just allowed us to grow." In addition, another owner imparted, "So back in 2011, we started making a formal plan, well I say formal, we started making a plan with financial and cross training roles, within the company." A systematic plan provides stability for the CEO or owner by having internal employees ready to backfill any critical needs. By having family and nonfamily members understanding the family history of an FOB, this will enhance collaboration, allowing the owner to think more strategically about his or her exit and feel confident that his legacy will be honored by the next generation.

Your Time to Reflect:

- *What lessons did you learn from your parents? Grand-parents? Do you share stories of your parents, grandparents, or great-grandparents?*
- *What are some of your family traditions? How do you highlight your family history?*
- *Do you have pictures of the founders in your business? If so, where are they? If not, why not? Do you have their names displayed in the boardrooms?*
- *Is all your paperwork in order? Have you been selling or gifting shares to your children? Have you identified who the next family or nonfamily member will be to lead the FOB?*

CHAPTER 6

ORGANIZATIONAL CULTURE,
VALUES, AND NORMS

Organizational culture is thought of as a complex set of ideologies and values shared throughout a business which influences how the business conducts itself and develops its employees. This is especially a relevant concern for FOBs (Lavie, 2006; Stevens, 2008). When a business loses its culture, it threatens its overall performance and how the FOB achieves its overall goals (Pindado & Requejo, 2015). Loss of organizational culture is a source of conflict between owners and employees, so exploring ways to maintain organizational culture in succession planning transition is critical in FOBs.

Without an adequate succession planning transition in place, a business loses its organizational culture, identity, and reputation. This loss negatively impacts its customer loyalty and market share, thereby decreasing the business's ability to survive to the next generation (Obadan & Ohiorenoya, 2013). Maintaining organizational culture during succession planning transition is clearly of the highest importance in FOBs. If businesses do not have a successful succession transition in place that trains the next generation about the culture, mission, vision, and goals that make up the foundation of the company, the business runs the risk of losing all that it has spent time, resources, and money developing. Effective succession management provides long-term sustainability of the business and its culture and ensures that capable and trained employees are in the business to take leadership positions when selected (Onwuka et al., 2017).

Knowing the organizational culture, values, and norms includes identifying the different activities that the CEOs or owners establish to help develop and maintain the culture of the FOB. CEOs or owners build relationships with their family and employees, both family and nonfamily, to develop an understanding that maintains the FOB's culture, values, and norms. Knowing the organizational culture, values, and norms includes communicating the timeline of events for an owner's exit, discussing whether the future incumbent would be a family or nonfamily member, and working with senior leadership on the goals to be accomplished before his or her tenure is up.

Many participants in my study who observed their children being productive at work and treating employees with respect and dignity were more likely willing to walk away and think about slowing down or retiring. Having values is important for FOBs to establish a foundational roadmap for family and nonfamily members to follow and live by when they are at work. If values are established in the first generation and then passed on, this would preserve the legacy of the CEOs or owners. When employees live the culture, values, and norms of the FOB, this positively influences how they interact with customers, vendors, and other employees.

Numerous participants agreed that as the CEOs or owners, they influenced the culture of the FOB by being transparent, engaging themselves, and seeing to the emotional well-being of the employees. One participant stated, "Yes, I personally communicated to my leadership team and others that I'm going to be the CEO, and I'm going to be around the next five years. It takes a long time to plan these big leadership shifts." Another owner confirmed, "We have truly developed a family culture, and the employees respond by being engaged. We take care of our employees when they are in need, and again they respond with being faithful and loyal to the FOB." Furthermore, another participant responded, "My vision for succession is that companies die and wither if they don't have fresh young blood to reinvigorate the system ... everybody's treated with respect and compassion ... we do everything by our core values." Leading by example, these participants lived, and then expected from employees, the FOB's organizational culture, values, and norms.

Some participants made an investment in their FOB by bringing in professionals to help the family understand the importance of the culture, values, and norms. For the next generation to learn those important lessons and help employees develop a solid foundation to enhance their skills, participants relied on the skills of coaches, mentors, and supervisors. One of the participants affirmed that when the CEOs or owners had the vision of the future to find the right professionals, this prepared employees for future leadership opportunities and developed a sense of what was important, helping to drive the organizational culture, values, and norms.

> I began to have coaching done for my family, for my niece, and my two sons. I also began to have coaching, as I said, done for other people in the team. And that encouraged, I think, the conversation about individual members of the executive team and what should happen after them. And so, the concept of, I think for me, succession planning is not just thinking about who, but thinking about when and what you want as a successor.

The owners of an FOB need to be fair, firm, and consistent with the organizational culture, values, and norms of their business, and they need to be very transparent with themselves, their family, and any trusted senior leader who they consider as family. One participant claimed that if the leadership wished to transition the business to one person in their family or to another senior leader for that matter, their requests needed to be clearly documented and explained to the family.

> My father was explaining to the president that I would be coming to work at the company, and the president said, before my dad could explain what role I would be in, "I would be happy to work for your daughter." And

my dad said, "No, actually, she's going to be working underneath you in this role.

Another participant included, "I think it was good, but again, it was so slow. It was over literally two decades from the time I started until the time I took over. There wasn't any clear defining moment of oh, dad's out, I'm in." This participant indicated that when the successor and the incumbent started very early in the transition process, the employees were less likely to notice the change in guard and instead focused on the organizational culture, values, and norms of the FOB.

Some participants imparted that when FOBs had numerous locations in various areas of the world, they needed to educate their employees about the diverse cultures and the communities in which they operated. Some of those participants also needed to allow their employees the opportunities to volunteer their time and services to support those communities. By providing both money and time for the causes that are important to the local communities and to the employees, they reinforce the organizational culture, values, and norms of the FOB. When culture, values, and norms are written down in a clear manner, this can help both family and nonfamily employees understand how they will need to act and perform within the FOB.

In family-owned businesses, the culture, values, and norms are usually developed by the first-generation owner and passed down by what I call "tribal knowledge" to the next generations. I encourage owners of FOBs to have clear values and norms to be shared and passed down to both family and nonfamily employees. I am happy to share my values, which I genuinely believe I have because of my father and his father, etc.

My values include:

Education – I learn and read something new every day. Once I master that, I then go teach it to someone else.

Professionalism – I always strive to be an upstanding citizen and do my best to deliver a quality output and deliverables to my customers.

Integrity – I am always truthful to others and myself.

Teamwork – I sacrifice myself for the greater good of the team, unless it is illegal, immoral, or unethical.

Compassion –I always defend the weak and speak up for those who cannot do it for themselves.

Fitness – I work my body every day to be physically fit.

Family – I never lose sight of what is truly important. I love my wife and my daughters. I will always honor my mother and father. It is one of the 10 commandments!

Loyalty – I am always true to the ones I serve and to my friends.

Humor – I make people laugh to lighten the mood and their burdens.

Gratitude – I am always thankful for what I have. I am also thankful for any good or bad experience because both have helped me be the person I am.

Your Time to Reflect:

- *What are the most important values to you in your business? What are some of your values in your personal life? Do you see comparisons or inconsistencies with personal and business values?*
- *What problems are you and your business trying to overcome now?*

- *Do you have your culture, values, and norms written out?*
- *What is your owner passionate about, and how do you know this?*
- *Do both family and nonfamily employees understand the norms of working for the FOB?*

CHAPTER 7

———— ◦ ⟷ ◦ ————

MENTORING

I consider my father one of the best mentors I had and am so blessed to have learned from him. His lessons were professional both at work and at home. I have also heard many stories from employees of his various stores about how he would go out of his way to take someone under his wing. My father had this unofficial mentor strategy, and it was through lessons learned through books, his own life experiences, professional networks, and just good old hard work from on-the-job training that he was able to positively impact so many people. This was my father's way of passing on that knowledge.

I also would like to honor my mother, Sheila P. Kerzner. I spelled her first name wrong in my dissertation, so I better make sure twice that I spell her name correctly in this book. ☺ I have the bug of teaching and passing on the knowledge that I learn, and this is a direct result of my mother's influence. Being a teacher, she reinforced the importance of education, and through her unending support and confidence in me, she encouraged me to push myself. She also installed the value of remembering what is important, such as family and friends. My mother taught me lessons of integrity and the importance of not being judgmental. She also motivated me to embrace my curious mindset. She also said to not be afraid to ask the universe for what you want. The worst thing that can happen is you hear the answer "no", and then, you find another way.

Mom mentoring two generations of women in our family

I believe it is important to share with you my teaching philosophy and how I work with students and those I mentor.

My Teaching Philosophy (Statement)

My teaching philosophy combines experiential learning with a strong emphasis on critical thinking and problem solving to help students develop independent, analytical thought processes which they can apply in all aspects of their lives. As I believe that experience can often be the best teacher, I frequently share stories from my own background as a consultant and human resource professional to engage students in real-life business situations that they may encounter during their careers. My teaching philosophy emphasizes the principle of when you teach, you learn. When a student has an opportunity to learn a model or theory and teach others how it is used and implemented, that will reinforce his or her learning journey.

I also believe that in the study of human resources, transparent communication skills are critical. I utilize the Socratic Method in my teaching and prompt my students to ask questions of themselves and others to strive to get to the root cause to better understand the matter at hand. As part of my course curriculum, I require my students to keep journals and capture lessons learned by all who are in the course. I find this journal activity not only keeps the students engaged and participating, but also develops active listening and teamwork to help them be future leaders.

I have a vast array of experience regarding mentoring, advising, and providing work experience with students from diverse backgrounds. Over the course of thirteen years teaching at the University of New Haven, I taught several international students from China, India, Saudi Arabia, Israel, Egypt, South Africa, Haiti, Japan, and Mexico. I fondly remember a student from China in one of my courses while I was a Director of Human Resources for an international company. I gave this student an internship and mentored him in human resources, and I learned so much from him about Chinese culture. The internship led to a full-time position post-graduation for my student in Shanghai, China. Please see some examples of the comments my past students have posted to my LinkedIn account to get a sense of my teaching/leadership style and how I mentored them both in and outside of the classroom.

Ruoyang Yan
凯华公司 - Senior HR Generalist
August 3, 2015

"Matt is a great leader and mentor who knows how to provide guidance and freedom to do different things to the early young professionals. I feel so lucky to be able to know him and start my career with him."

Marco Baratta, M.A.
Regional Human Resources Manager at YKK EL SALVADOR
April 15, 2010

"I found Matthew approach to HR theory and his classes highly inspirational, Mathew is one of the best teachers I ever had, he had the ability to make the Human Resources theory come alive through his great real-life examples from his experience. He managed the class in a way that a synergism was created in which student's participation and theory melt, from which the learning experience reached its maximum approach. Mathew made us think about our lives and how those relate to the human potential we have to unleash from employees in organizations. This is how he finished the last class I attended with him: "Human resources is not the book that you bought, and not the fact that we are going to get over class lessons, throw that away! and think of we deal with human beings, and getting to know people, it's the highest form of motivation and if you have a problem in the organization or things are broken and you need to fix them and you are the consultant or the IO Psychologist or you are the MBA wizard who is going to come and fix them, remember if you want to help the bottom line, get to know your people, because people will get to help the bottom line…" A true gift for any student.

I share this feedback from my past students/mentees to show how the lessons I learned from my past generations impact me and continue to impact me as a working professional and all-around good individual.

As a result, I feel that I am positively impacting the future by passing on this knowledge to others.

Throughout my journey of family business advising and researching, there is a remarkably interesting story. Earlier in this book, you read about how and why I wanted to research and study succession planning in family business, but what I did not tell you then is how I landed my job working in a field I love. When I was in my third year of my PhD studies, we had to take our exams before we were allowed to defend our proposal and submit that into the Independent Review Board (IRB). During the exam time frame, we (the members of my cohort) had to put our problem statement, purpose, and data methodology on display so that other peers and professors could comment and offer input. Well, one of my peers, Yvonne Kinney, Ph.D., read my topic and told me that I needed to reach out to a person named Lisë Stewart. I was so burnt out from the exams that I could not focus. My friend returned and said, "I noticed you did not write her name down. Lisë Stewart is her name, and she is the "family whisperer."

After hearing the words "family whisperer", I quickly wrote down Lisë's name. It took me about two, maybe three weeks to track her down, but I am so happy that I did. During the first call, we spoke for a good, solid hour-and-a-half about family succession, my proposed study, and the work that Lisë does. I immediately felt very comfortable and asked Lisë if she would be my mentor, as we were encouraged to find experts in the field we were studying. Lisë asked if she could have some time to think about it and asked if we could schedule another call. Two weeks later, we had another, wonderful hour-and-a-half call, discussing more of the consulting work that she does in the family business world. I also learned that Lisë ran a non-profit organization that trained business advisors on how to work with family businesses. Lisë asked if I would be interested in taking her upcoming course, and I jumped at the opportunity.

The stars were aligned even more so. On day two of the three-day course, Lisë had to take a prospective client call during lunch. She approached me after her call and said, "Matt, I know we are getting to know each other, but I have a request for you. I have a prospective client who is looking for family business strategy work, but he is also having labor relations and HR issues. I do not have that background, so would you be interested in partnering up with me on this consulting project?" I had a good amount of personal time off (PTO) at my job and said I would soak this up as an internship. I was ecstatic to have this opportunity to work with the "family whisperer".

In short, this consulting job was an extreme success and led to a few more opportunities in short order. I ran into a little dilemma because I exhausted my PTO time, and the consulting work kept on being introduced to me when I received that call from Lisë. She informed me that she was selling her book of business to an accounting firm to start a Center for Family Business and asked if I would be interested in working for her. I did not have to think twice to answer that question. Now, 6 years later, I am watching Lisë transition with dignity and honor her past, live her impressive present, and plan for her best future. She has helped me transition and develop practical skills, pre-and post-doctorate. Lisë is a true mentor, and I am blessed that she has been helping me reach my dreams.

Speaking engagement day 2 of my job

When conducting research for my study, it was clear that owners thought strategically about how they developed and managed their talent. The definition of talent management relates to how businesses reward and recognize their highly talented employees. However, there is a lack of clarity concerning the definition of talent management and how it could be used with succession planning transition (Lewis & Heckman, 2006).

There is a set of human resource practices within a business that are to be followed to help predict and support the flow of human capital based on skills, knowledge, and ability (Lewis & Heckman, 2006). Talent management is used to reward employees who are identified as high potential employees, those who succeed in their current positions and keep growing and assuming more responsibility within a business. Managing talent within a business is important because if leaders seek talent outside the business, internal talent might see this as a threat, undermining teamwork and increasing turnover (Pfeffer, 2001).

When owners use coaching and mentoring, they are developing the next generation of leaders. Coaching is incredibly significant and relevant to the succession planning transition to help give successors in key positions opportunities to seek guidance and develop the expertise to step in when needed by the business. If owners utilize coaching as a continuous learning tool, they will be more prepared to make succession decisions in a timelier fashion and stay within the business when a position needs to be filled. Also, if incumbents use coaching, they are teaching coaching skills to the next generation to help develop their future successors.

If owners of FOBs have capable family members in the right positions, not only would they stay competitive in the market, but they would also have a qualified bench that is ready and willing to take over if, and when, they need to transition. If owners have their children and other family members working for them, the owners need to make sure they have the proper tools in place to teach the skills and knowledge the family members would need to contribute to the business. Thus, owners who invest in developing their family members help a succession process because it allows for the development of an individualized plan to enhance the family members' skills and talents which could be used to strengthen the FOB. If family members have specific roles and responsibilities within the FOB, this reduces any conflicts or communication breakdown that interferes with the succession transition of who is the next in line to assume leadership positions.

Developing nonfamily employees is also especially important to the succession planning transition because the family may have only a limited number of family members who work for the business. Owners develop nonfamily members because they may have family working within the company but do not have the leadership characteristics to run the business. Owners of FOBs who recognize that nonfamily members are key to the survival of their business could impact not only the financial bottom line of the profit and loss statement, but they could look at some of these employees in key positions to be part of the succession process, keeping the continuity of the FOB when they experience turnover with some key leadership positions.

Taking time to hire family and nonfamily members properly is one of the most important decisions and responsibilities an owner makes. An owner needs to learn how to be a coaching manager/leader and spend quality time developing any employee he sees as a possible successor. A coaching manager is someone who uses coaching to develop talent to obtain the results he needs (Hunt & Weintraub, 2016). Leadership needs to understand the importance of providing training and development to help support the succession planning transition with the correct leadership competencies.

Researchers report that as businesses compete in a more global marketplace, leaders need to think about their businesses and the shortage of potential leaders among their current workforce and the need to develop the training for those employees who have the proper skills, knowledge, and ability to be considered for leadership positions (Copland, 2001). When coaching and skill development are used in which the leader shares his experiences with the successor, positive results occur, including the identification of the competencies needed for the employees to develop the skills, knowledge, and capabilities to achieve the leadership performance (Samei & Feyzbakhsh, 2016). Additionally, sharing feedback during coaching significantly helps in improving the successor's managerial and technical knowledge and skills to take over as the leader (Samei & Feyzbakhsh, 2016). Thus, it is evident that leaders must have the critical skill set of being able to train and develop their next generation (Adedayo, Olanipekun & Ojo, 2016).

In making hiring decisions, participants focused on finding talent for their FOBs by looking at promotional opportunities for existing employees. Participants also evaluated their current bench strength to identify the skill sets they needed when looking for talent and hiring talent from outside the FOB. By promoting from within, one participant affirmed he did not have to teach the organizational culture, values, and norms of their FOB, reducing the amount of time, or learning curve, for the incumbent.

> As an owner, I like to promote people from within the organization. There are times we have promoted people into positions that they were not yet qualified to be in. But we find if we coach, mentor them, and provide the tools they need, eventually they will do a great job for us. We find that when people are promoted from within, they understand our culture of the FOB, and this can help us succeed. It is important to know that whatever gaps the employee has, we need to work with them to close them so they can be comfortable in their new role.

In making hiring decisions, several participants constantly reviewed and discussed the bench strength of those employees who were either backups or had potential to backfill any key positions within the business. When a key employee leaves the FOB, it is advantageous if the FOB has qualified employees to quickly replenish existing positions. One participant offered, "We all know the key people, like we discussed earlier, that we can't lose, we always try to have a backstop for them and we're constantly talking about the people that we might be vulnerable with." In addition, another owner proclaimed, "I would think about, well, when would they be leaving if at all, and who would be behind them and what should be the process by which we think about that?"

With employees who are trained and qualified to immediately step in, FOBs are prepared throughout the transition process. When CEOs or owners spend time developing their employees to understand the behaviors they want, this can help drive a leadership and ownership culture.

Your Time to Reflect:

- *Do you have a formal mentoring program? Informal?*
- *What are your short-term goals? Long-term goals?*
- *What interests you about having a mentor or mentee?*
- *Do you have a list of competencies you want the mentored employees to follow?*
- *What skills do you want to develop?*

CHAPTER 8

◆━━◆◆◇◆◆━━◆

PROTECTING EMPLOYEES

When employees understand how they need to perform in the workplace, this can make all the difference. Employees who feel comfortable and safe in the FOB are more motivated and engaged. Protecting employees includes developing protocols and processes to help maintain a work environment, allowing employees to be able to participate and feel valued. To protect employees, there are activities to help maintain the FOB's culture, values, and norms. In my research study, several participants asserted that to help maintain culture, they attended orientations to say hello, meet, and greet the new employees. One participant stated, "When we have a new employee, we meet them as soon as they come in the door. We basically kind of give a little bit of an overview of the culture and have a personal conversation with them." Protecting employees includes the opportunity to share the culture, values, and norms of the business.

Throughout the study, many participants remarked that clear communication was vital to the success of their FOB. One business owner stated, "Having a daily meeting with my team and reviewing the daily agenda helps communicate what our priorities are for the day. By doing this meeting every day, it helps set the culture of the company that communication is very important." Another owner contributed to this thought by saying that when CEOs or owners set the expectation that communication was a critical part of their organizational health, it reinforced the importance of following the culture, values, and norms projected by the CEO or owner of the FOB.

> Every day at 10:30, there's a conference call, and there's probably 21 people on the conference call. The main reason for the conference call is the transportation team. The conference call lasts an hour every day. We basically go over the whole agenda. What's interesting is all the key managers are also on this call for the most part at every plant because transportation's such a huge part of our business. So, we've been doing this now for 10 years, and when you have the owners on the phone for an hour, hour-and-a-half every day, all these managers, they're really getting indoctrinated about how things should be done.

It was refreshing to notice that most participants led by example. These participants proclaimed that they worked hard, side-by-side with their employees, to help drive the work ethic and culture of the FOB. When participants showed their employees that they were willing to roll up their sleeves and participate in the daily tasks, employees saw firsthand that the CEOs or owners cared about the work that was being produced, and they were actively involved with their FOBs. One leader stated that earning the respect of his employees and treating them like family were key components of his FOB.

> Well, we care very much for the business. And I think, being a family business and being so involved in the business, and not only just being owner, but working with the people ... We're not sitting there watching them work. We're working with them. And I think that people see that, and they respect us differently for that. Yes... I'm not, we're not silent owners.

It was evident that CEOs or owners of FOBs could not compromise their values and what they had built. Participants relayed that it was important to tell stories to employees about the values of the business and how important it was not to violate them. One participant shared this experience by valuing clear communication and having conversations about the organizational culture, values, and norms to protect both their employees and the FOB.

> We try to be consistent with those values. And we try to communicate our values. Well, I try to live it and that's the best way... I do a monthly newsletter called the State of the Union in which I tell people exactly what I think is happening... I try to communicate and overcommunicate. I always think that knowledge is power. And I try to be as transparent as possible, so everybody knows what we're doing.

After speaking with the 15 participants, I also learned that CEOs or owners needed to educate their workforce about their culture on their first day of employment. One owner stated, "We hope to kind of keep pushing that by reminding people of what those core values are, and we do that through orientation. We do that through annual reviews ... we talk a little bit about the culture of the company." Understanding culture drives the message that CEOs or owners care about the foundation of the business and what it represents, and when this is done at the onset of one's career, the message is clear to the employees that this theme matters.

Multiple participants commented that taking care of employee needs was important in their FOBs. By protecting employees on various levels, participants demonstrated their commitment to provide a safe and welcoming environment, and in turn, employees worked hard to show their appreciation. In following suit of understanding family history and knowing the business's culture, values, and norms, one participant revealed that he viewed his employees as more than just employees.

So, we really are passionate about taking care of our own. So, we do extra things or go the extra mile for employees who might be having a tough time, even in their personal lives. I have several examples of employees we've helped in difficult situations. Because it's been throughout our company culture, through my grandfather and my dad, that we show we care for people.

One participant also shared, "We also have an EAP. If it's a personal issue that they're really struggling with, or if it's bleeding over to work, we have an Employee Assistance Program that they can utilize." By offering services to protect and maintain our most important assets, the employees in turn will feel safe and encouraged to take care of the internal and external customers. This is one of the major lessons I learned while working at Stop & Shop.

Your Time to Reflect:

- *Do you have an employee handbook?*
- *Do you have written policies and procedures?*
- *How often do you review or change a policy or procedure? What policies should you have for your family employees? nonfamily?*
- *Is your Human Resource manager trained to work with both family and nonfamily members?*
- *Do you have a process where you allow your nonfamily employees to have a voice?*

CHAPTER 9

———•◦❧◦•———

ADVOCATES AND TRUSTED ADVISORS

My father did not come up with his plans for a successful liquidity event by himself. He had several advisors, both family and professionals, to help educate him on his path. My father used an attorney, his wealth advisor, CPA, family business advisor, a venture capitals banker, and his trusted siblings to help. I watched my father choose his advisors wisely and use them frequently in a way to help him work through some of the emotional decisions he had to make. He needed to get their sound advice without any of the entanglements with which he was wrestling.

There are four important advocates within FOBs who directly influence the succession planning transition. The first one is the incumbent, the owner and the family member holding the senior leadership position who is ready and willing to relinquish his or her position to a new family member (Bozer, Levin, & Santora, 2017). Researchers recognize that the incumbent identity is linked to the FOB, and this reflects in the business's culture and norms (Bozer et al., 2017). For an FOB to be successful, both the incumbent and successor need to take an active interest in activities outside of the business; this is instrumental in allowing the succession planning transition to take place between the incumbent and the successor (Cabrera-Suárez, De Saá-Perez, & García-Almeida, 2001).

The second advocate, the successor, is the family member who is chosen and has taken over the leadership position from the incumbent (Bozer et al., 2017). Successors of FOBs are incredibly supportive of having early exposure to the family business, and research shows a positive commitment to taking on the leadership positions (Klein, Astrachan, & Smyrnios, 2005). Researchers report that successors have greater benefit and understanding of their roles and responsibilities working within their FOBs rather than working outside of the FOB and then returning (Barach, Carson, & Doochin, 1988). FOBs need to make investments in their human capital, which may include allowing family member employees to leave other businesses, if there are any, to provide other educational tasks, such as mentoring, coaching, and teambuilding within the FOB (Renkert-Thomas, 2016).

The third advocates are considered the family members in the FOB who are involved in developing or maintaining family values, strategic goals, and daily management activities (Frank, Kessler, Rusch, Suess-Reyes, & Weismeier-Sammer, 2016). Family members who do not directly work in the business still play a critical role with how the family acts in and around the community of the operating business. Highly engaged family members straddle the often-competing needs of both the family and the business and provide a vital link in ensuring that family values and goals are incorporated in business planning. Family members include both family members who work for the FOB or family members who understand the mission, vision, and values of the family business without being directly employed there. Because those individuals understand the foundation of the FOB, they add value to help grow the business and provide operational strategies. Like developing key employees, having family members in an FOB provides a level of trust and respect that may not be found in nonfamily employees. One business owner offered his opinion for this topic by stating:

> We learned to respect each other. We trust our customers
> very well, but at times we forget how to treat each other.
> Just like family, there are times we take each other for

granted. We need to learn and do a better job at treating each other within the FOB with respect.

Other participants in the study supported this idea of open communication and learning from the past. When CEOs or owners have trusted people to talk to, they serve as a sounding board and foster a safe environment to bounce ideas and plans. If appropriately engaged in the transition, they could bring an important dynamic to the succession conversation.

Finally, the nonfamily members are the fourth key advocates. These supporters are nonrelated employees who work for the FOB and possess the skills, knowledge, and abilities that other advocates do not (Chrisman, Chua, Sharma, & Yoder, 2009). This group of advocates is critical to the future success of the business, as some may not become identified as future leaders, but nonetheless, play a significant role in the business. They bring historical knowledge, technical expertise, an understanding of organizational culture, and the unique perspective of nonfamily employees.

Trusted advisors are key employees, external resources, and family members who hold the CEO or owner accountable, provide sound feedback, and bring a diverse set of skills that are needed to help make critical decisions before, during, and after a succession planning transition (Davis, Dibrell, Craig, & Green, 2013; Reay, Pearson, & Gibb, 2013; Strike, 2012). Having trusted advisors helps the CEO or owner think through and make critical business decisions, such as role clarification, high potential identification, and succession planning processes. When CEOs and owners use trusted advisors, this helps them look at business functions and family dynamics in a more objective manner.

Having trusted advisors who understand the roles and responsibilities during a transition helps CEOs and owners identify the gaps that are needed currently and in the future. Trusted advisors can include the Board of Directors, Accountants, Attorneys, Family Business Advisors, Key employees, and Family Business Advisors. When every player on the team understands what is expected of him or her and how to work within the FOB, this supports organizational health and employee engagement. It is the CEO or owner's responsibility to teach and train his children to take over the FOB, and he or she needs to play mentor and coach them to learn. There also needs to be a backup plan for the successor. It is good practice to have understudies learning the job and provide the CEO or owner with options in case the first choice does not work out.

External resources are content experts who understand both the internal politics and the external landscape of the FOB to provide strategic direction and include Family Business Advisors, Personal Financial Planners, Attorneys, Insurance Brokers, CPAs, and Business Valuation Experts. Although they do not work directly for the business, these individuals provide guidance to the CEO or owner. In utilizing external resources, several participants revealed that it was satisfying to find quality employees who wanted to take on more responsibility and could move up in the FOB. One participant declared, "I've been very fortunate to find a strategic planning director, which was phenomenal for a leader to have somebody that's really good at that detail process." Another owner added, "Talking about succession planning with my advisor is very healthy and helps me make some good decisions. I like to see how I am performing on a daily basis and the contribution I am making to the organization." When family business owners find the right cultural fit for an advisor, this can make the world of difference in reducing the resistance of putting a succession plan in place.

As FOBs grow in size and revenue, it is helpful to bring in external resources to help run the business or specific departments. The CEOs or owners need to pay them accordingly, so they feel they are part of the growth and development and could share the success of the development of the company. One participant commented, "The business has nearly doubled in size over the last six or seven years. What used to be fairly easy for my mom and my brother and I to manage really hands on, we simply cannot manage hands on." External resources provide the needed professionalism, commitment, and attention to businesses throughout, and after, the succession planning transition.

Your Time to Reflect:

- *Do you have family members who you consider to be sounding boards? Do you have individuals you trust to seek advice and counsel regarding your succession planning process?*
- *Do you have a few key employees who you consider to be part of your inner circle who can help tell the story of the FOB and who can help provide honest feedback and guidance to both senior leaders and family members?*
- *What are your advisors' qualifications? How will your relationship work with those advisors?*
- *Do you have external resources to help provide feedback and guidance regarding family, business, and ownership matters?*

CHAPTER 10

ORGANIZATIONAL HEALTH AND STRATEGIC DEVELOPMENT

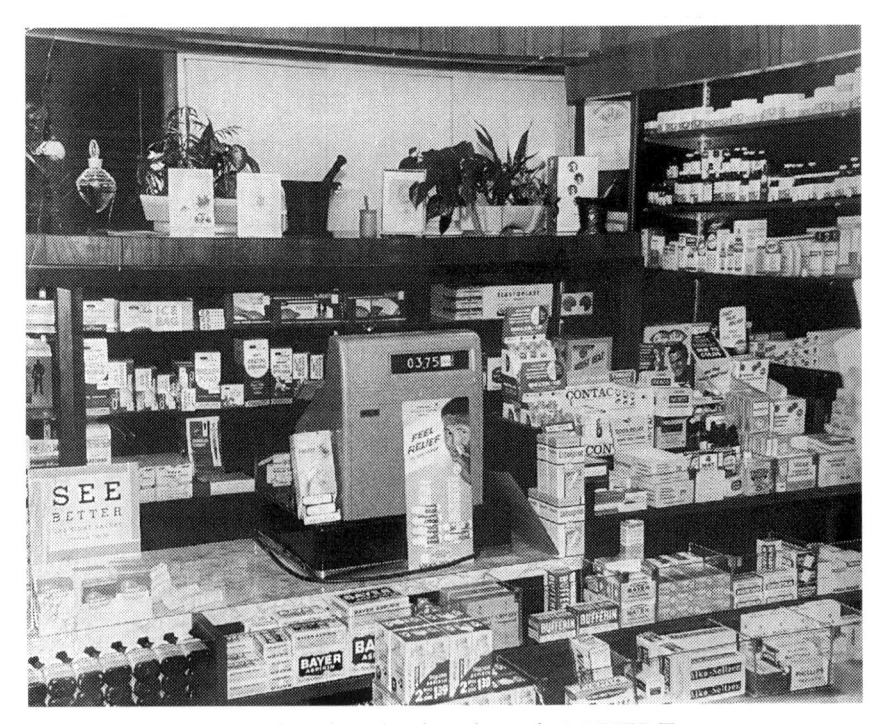

Merchandise displayed inside MiKERZ

My father was always thinking about different ways to increase his footprint and profitability by introducing new products and services to his business. If you ever walked into MiKERZ, you would see that he used every inch of retail space for merchandise. It was amazing to see how many different items he sold in his little kingdom. I raise this point because he felt that if he maximized his offerings and services, he would stay competitive and have an advantage over his competitors who were also in his trade space. He was always looking to do this better and in a way that would bring him efficiency. My father, as I mentioned earlier, taught and mentored young pharmacists and young adults in the business, and he did so with energy, passion, and with a mindset of continuous improvement. Everyone understood his or her roles and responsibilities, and no work was too little or too great for anyone.

Organizational health refers to the ability of a business to align, execute, and renew itself faster than its competition. Organizational health not only targets a business's financial sustainability, but also increases its operational profits and develops its employees to meet the challenges of the competitive landscape. An example of organizational health occurs when business owners learn from their mistakes and continuously improve their ability to compete in unique ways that competition could not copy (Mushref & Al-Jabiri, 2017). Researchers demonstrate that strong organizational health propels a business's performance and helps its leaders create a path of continued improvement (Keller & Price, 2011). For an FOB to have and maintain organizational health, the business must have a good understanding of the external environment in which it operates, and it must have a passion for understanding the capabilities of its workforce as it relates to organizational performance.

According to MacIntosh (2007), the concept of organizational health first appeared in literature over 40 years ago. Warren Bennis (1962) was one of the first theorists to introduce organizational health as a way to organizational effectiveness and presented the three dimensions of organizational health as adaptability, coherence of identity, and the ability to perceive the world. A business that sustains its organizational health yields more powerful assets and generates total returns to shareholders 3 times higher than unhealthy businesses (DeSmet & Pohlmeyer, 2013).

According to DeSmet & Pohlmeyer (2013), there are four leader-driven practices that help sustain organizational health, and when implemented, businesses are 5 times more likely to be healthy and deliver strong performances over those businesses without strong practices in place. These practices include high potential leaders who could determine how to deliver results and are also held accountable to achieve them. These are the businesses that have a strong market focus and a good handle on the external orientation toward not only customers, but all stakeholders, both internally and externally. These businesses have the execution edge, strive for continuous improvement, and raise quality and productivity while eliminating waste and inefficiency. Additionally, these types of businesses search for talent and encourage building a competitive advantage by assembling and managing quality skills and a knowledge base.

Researchers state that the most difficult task for both FOBs and NFOBs is to achieve a competitive edge from developing its employees through improved organizational capability (Prahalad & Hamel, 2006; Ulrich & Lake, 1990). This refers to the internal development of internal policies, procedures, and processes that help support proper behaviors to maintain the business's competitive advantage and the needs of all internal and external stakeholders (Reid & Adams, 2001).

A successful business utilizes intangible resources, a set of capabilities, and core competencies to enhance its intellectual and system capabilities and ensure a more competitive advantage than just having physical assets (Quinn, Anderson, & Finkelstein, 1996). Intellectual and system capabilities address the business's capacity to manage human intellect and to convert it into useful products and services (Quinn et al., 1996). When FOBs develop their human resource practices and procedures around organizational health, specifically in talent development, this helps the owners have confidence in both their family and nonfamily employees when thinking about succession planning. According to researchers, there is a strong correlation between organizational health and both operational success and financial performance (DeSmet & Pohlmeyer, 2013).

When owners in FOBs increase communication with their employees about the strategic direction of the company, trust is built. Trust is a key element to organizational health as it is critical for the long-term survival of a business. When owners share knowledge, both formally and informally, about the direction of their businesses, all stakeholders, employees, customers, and suppliers have a sense of confidence and trust that the business is performing. This trust is called knowledge-based trust and is trust that is grounded in knowledge about another party and developed through repeated interactions (Holsappke & Wu, 2008).

According to Keller and Price (2011), organizational health is viewed through five frames to help businesses reach their ultimate, competitive advantage over their competitors. By using the five frames of organizational health regarding succession planning, owners have a standard process to clearly communicate desired outcomes and lead the business to a successful transition. These five frames are Aspire, Assess, Architect, Act, and Advance (see Table 7). These five frames have associated health imperatives that businesses employ to maximize organizational health.

Table 7

Five Frames of Performance and Health (Keller & Price, 2011)

Frame	Health Imperative
1. Aspire: Where do we want to go?	Determine what "healthy" looks like for the business.
2. Assess: How ready are we to go there?	Uncover the root cause of mindsets that support or undermine organizational health.
3. Architect: What must we do to get there?	Reshape the work environment to create healthy mindsets.

| 4. | Act: How do we manage the journey? | Ensure that energy for change is continually infused and unleashed. |

| 5. | Advance: How do we keep moving forward? | Equip leaders to lead from core of self-mastery. |

The first frame, Aspire, asks where the business wants to go. In this frame, the business leaders need to determine what healthy looks like for them and how they want to convey that message to the employees. Within the context of succession planning, business leaders consider if the definition of healthy would change or remain the same throughout, and after, the transition process.

The second frame is Assess, and in this frame, the business leaders need to determine their readiness to get to where the business wants to go. Here, it is important for them to uncover the root cause of mindsets that both support and/or undermine organizational health. In this frame, FOBs undergoing succession planning consider what mindsets and capabilities align most closely with their objectives to achieve their overall performance goals before, and after, succession planning and leadership change.

The third frame is Architect, and here the business leaders consider what they must do to obtain the desired result they want. In this frame, the leaders reshape their work environment to develop healthy mindsets that facilitate organizational health. This could be accomplished by changing any formal systems, structures, processes, and incentives (Keller & Price, 2011).

The fourth frame is Act. In this frame, the business leaders need to answer how they carry out the action steps to manage the journey and create the change towards organizational health. Healthy businesses use pilot programs to start initiatives and to ensure that energy for change is continually infused and unleashed.

In the fifth and final frame, Advance, the business leaders need to answer how they keep moving forward to maintain the continuous change needed to maximize the competitive advantage. It is important that they provide their executives the tools that are needed to lead the business from a core of self-mastery (Keller & Price, 2011). Here, the business leaders further develop tools that support knowledge sharing, learning opportunities, employee growth, and bench strength at all levels of the business to identify continuous improvement before, during, and after succession planning.

Researchers point out that organizational health is how employees perceive a sense of justice with how owners of FOBs make decisions (Shoaf, Genaidy, Karwowski, & Huang, 2005). Employees need to have a perception that there is justice, as perceived justice and organizational health have a positive impact on job attitudes within businesses (Barnett & Kellermanns, 2006). Researchers also note that there is a need for a commitment to fairness, which could be established by identifying clarity in communication, consistency, and change as essential features of a decision-making process (Greenberg & Cropanzano, 1993; Leventhal, 1980). Researchers state the difficulty of any application of distributive justice within the FOB is that family, shareholders, and nonfamily employees judge fairness and organizational health with different criteria (Van der Heyde, Blondel, & Carlock, 2005). If employees perceive that there is a lack of distributive justice and fairness, this could have a negative impact on employee engagement, so perceptions of fairness are critical to the organizational health and the overall success of family-owned businesses.

I found that throughout my research study, strategic development for CEOs or owners related to the participants' experiences advancing the business to support financial sustainability and employee development. Strategic development includes having a workplace free from walls and offices to encourage open communication. Strategic development includes providing the proper training that allows employees to ask questions so CEOs or owners can get to the root cause of any issues. In using strategic development, CEOs or owners establish expectations, but they also provide feedback to the entire business concerning the business's sales and projections, methods to save money by introducing new technology and other ways to improve efficiency and the development of staff.

Growing the business is defined as developing revenue, products, and services. Various participants noted that when a new CEO or owner took over, he set new expectations for growing the business, introduced the right resources of people/talent, and provided them training and tools to position the business to grow in size and revenue. One participant commented that when a new CEO or owner resumed leadership, setting the expectations and developing goals for the FOB and all employees reinforced the commitment to the strategic development, ensuring the business continued to move in the right direction.

> I think that's really what made impactful engagement, just making sure that when we take over, we do have some different expectations, and this is a different animal than it was, even five years ago. We are going to go through different things. So, things are changing, so we have to change a little bit.

Engaged employees create a company that has good organizational health. When employees contribute to their department, they have an impact on the profit margins. Many participants pointed out that each employee made a difference if he became engaged and performed the jobs that were assigned to him. These participants stated that as employees became more knowledgeable at work because of their tenure, they added value by introducing different ideas for growing the business and saving the company money. One owner discussed this impact.

> But just net profits of the whole company are something that they can all impact. But they are impacted most significantly when they collaborate as different departments because obviously it's a matter of marketing and sales and food production and event operations and just general administration to really see the margins be where they should be on the net.

Multiple participants commented that employee morale was a key component of organizational health and employee development. When CEOs or owners acknowledge their employees and the special times in their lives, both personally and professionally, these simple acts improve employee morale. One participant reinforced this by affirming, "I think sometimes simple little things like also recognizing people's birthdays and anniversaries just takes the time to let people know that you thank them beyond the normal processes for their contributions to our success." Another owner pronounced, "I try to paint a fuller picture of people than just what you see at work." When participants take care of the personal needs of employees, this helps build loyalty to the business, and the employees perform better as a result.

CEOs or owners who have transparent communication with their workforce regarding succession planning for key positions support employees on numerous levels while also growing their business. When employees understand their roles and responsibilities and what positions are considered key, this develops an environment that promotes organizational health. Employees who feel comfortable with their superiors and engage in consistent, positive dialogue help the business grow and embrace the succession transition.

Many participants prepared for the future to help employees understand what was expected of them. One owner announced, "I think that because of the family meetings and because the board was involved, I think that it was a very transparent process. And I think that future successions, wherever those may be, I think being transparent is important." Transparent communication begins the process of having all the right people in the right positions doing their jobs, adding value to the FOB, and promoting good organizational health.

Those participants who are active listeners and ask for guidance from employees help drive the culture of the business. When incumbents are named, not everyone immediately trusts the judgment of the CEO or owner. Participants noted that open communication helped ease these feelings and started the discussion process. One participant expressed, "They come to me first. They haven't gone to dad for anything over the last couple of years. I have a good rapport, certainly not friends, but we're friendly." This participant articulated that there is a strong organizational culture where his employees and supervisors are comfortable communicating and seeking out his support and guidance, and not that of his father.

In business development, there are signs that show various participants that their business has good organizational health. Employees who go above and beyond doing their jobs and want to share ideas, ask for resources, and provide best practices show signs of engagement and add to the organizational health of the FOB. One owner asserted, "They'll stay late to finish. They take good pictures when they're done so we can put stuff on our website. They text you the night before with any concerns." When employees express interest exceeding the normal job responsibilities and take ownership in the outcome of the interactions with customers, this is a sign of positive organization health.

Customers are also important in the succession planning process. Multiple participants spent time with their customers to communicate the timing of the succession transition and develop a communication plan concerning the messages they wanted to send to the customers. Once the messages were sent, a visit to the customers with the incumbent was advantageous to help the transition process, allowing the customers to feel comfortable with the change. One business owner stated, "I think it's really important, of course, on the employee side, but there's so many other facets that transition affects…customers is a big one. And making sure that they feel comfortable with the transition is really important." Losing customers who are frustrated and unaware of the change in ownership is poor business and something that would not contribute to growing the business.

When participants were thinking about transitioning the business to the next generation, they needed to consider how the customers would react. If customers were given notice and were provided with some FAQs, this helped them feel more comfortable and prepared for the change in leadership. Many participants wanted to make customers feel that the process would be transparent and a nonevent for them. One owner needed his customers to be confident with the changes in leadership and know that it would be business as usual.

Some of our clients, I am sure, are going to be more reluctant. When I transition at some point, it will be a similar thing. There are some employees and clients and community members who will be sad to see me go and then not have the same level of trust, and whether it's my sister or my own children or some of my employees, there will be some of them who are excited to see me go because, I mean, I'm not without a few character flaws myself, I know I'm very dry, I'm very serious, I can be intimidating.

Participants noted that workers who had been employed for an extended period provided the business with a competitive advantage because their knowledge and experience stayed within the FOB. When employees leave, the knowledge and experience also leave. During the transition process, it is imperative that time is spent growing the business, not growing new employees.

FOBs with a high turnover rate tend to spend a lot of money in recruitment costs to replace employees, and at times, some CEOs or owners must start over educating the new employees. One participant supported this by saying, "These people have been around a long time. We realize how much trouble they can cause if they leave and go to a competitor. That's the only point I want to make." Some participants who were aware of tenured employees who might be flight risks engaged in conversation to understand dissatisfaction with the current state of their employment. Some of the participants also affirmed that an FOB that employed developing standard work practices captured employees' knowledge of skills and abilities in their current positions; accordingly, if they left the FOB, the employee knowledge would be memorialized within the FOB.

Numerous participants of FOBs looked at how they would be prepared for growth and what was needed to help maintain the stability for that growth. One owner asserted, "We were fortunate the market was right. Capital was available to borrow, we borrowed heavily, and there was a lot of sweat equity and US resources allocating that and growing the business." However, participants also recognized the need to invest in their employee growth and have the right amount of talent available, trained, and ready to expand for growing the business. Another participant offered, "The organization has grown at least tenfold since then. So, it's a little different situation and much more difficult to have the one-on-one mentoring like we did." When participants are growing their businesses, they also need to standardize their mentoring processes and develop their senior leaders to be surrogates, ready to step in and mentor the employees as though they are the CEOs or owners.

As the businesses grew in size and revenue, participants added more employees. With more employees, there was a need for more leaders to help manage the workforce. It was essential that employees who showed potential stepped up and led the growth of their FOBs. One leader declared that when his business provided leadership, training, and tools to learn and do the job, the sales numbers followed.

> It seems it took us 25 years to learn how to grow the business and get our employees ready for our growth period. It seems once we introduced learning and the tools for our employees, we saw tremendous growth in sales in the next 10 years. We went from 1 million in sales a year to 10 million in sales per year.

Many participants use different techniques to invest in their workforce, helping employees be prepared for their jobs and for their future. By investing in employees, this helps reduce turnover. Developing a retention plan is an effective way to retain key employees and address growing the business. Some retention programs invest in educating those key employees. In my study, I found that CEOs or owners developed an employee contract that had built-in incentives for reaching sales growth and the development of their teams. Multiple participants communicated that investing in an FOB was a priority. CEOs or owners needed to feel comfortable taking risks and use the appropriate resources and people to help achieve the goals originally established. One participant exclaimed that it was essential that CEOs or owners used the knowledge from past generations to determine what they would need for investing and growing their businesses.

> When I was younger, I watched my father take risks and invest in the FOB. It took me several years to learn the finances of the business to truly understand what my dad was doing to help grow the business. I am a lot more comfortable today to make calculated risks as my dad did. I would not have been able to do it or even understand it back then.

As mentioned earlier, continuous improvement is a process of looking at ways to make better use of tools and systems. When CEOs or owners set an expectation to complete an assignment to target continuous improvement, this helps increase employee engagement. Employees feel a sense of pride knowing that the CEO or owner trusts them to do the job.

In establishing continuous improvement, various participants pointed out that working in an FOB when methods were similar was satisfying; however, when family sibling business partners had different approaches, it became necessary to develop a code of conduct on how partners would work together and communicate to others. It was essential that employees heard one voice and one consistent message. If the partners did not agree on how they would work together, this caused frustration to the employees and was counterproductive for everyone. One owner stated, "Give them something to lead. A project that could be an event type thing where they're leading some sort of improvement. It could be giving the opportunity to lead just a team on a machine." Setting expectations, even at this management level, is a crucial step to achieving organizational health.

Many participants knew there were times when they needed to hire outside of the business. If the leaders were not confident that the current workforce could carry out the responsibilities established, or if employees did not wish to move up within the business, the CEOs or owners had to look elsewhere and find talent. One business owner communicated that he needed to spend the time to help capable employees build the confidence, not just the skills, so that they could be successful with a new job; in turn, employees needed to know that the FOB was there to support them in learning and establishing continuous improvement.

> And I think that there are times when perhaps we could go out and headhunt outside candidates with more unique expertise. And the other thing I think we've discovered as we've grown is that there were times, and I can think of a handful of instances, when we considered promoting from within, but were reluctant because some of the eligible candidates that we had within, we just didn't feel that they were old enough or experienced enough or skilled enough.

To target continuous improvement, participants put in systems to obtain market feedback, and employees were united in improving the operations and adhering to the strategic development of the FOB. Educating employees and procuring feedback about what new systems were introduced to the business helped increase the market share, helped develop a healthy bottom line, and helped increase organizational health. One participant commented, "I think that'd be a great area for improvement for me...I do like to watch the bottom line of where things are going and if I can invest in things that improve." When participants provided the tools for the employees to see current data, this developed open communication and presented opportunities for necessary dialogue to improve operational awareness in real time.

Throughout the study, I found that CEOs or owners who were aggressively looking to grow their business and even double in size in revenue growth acknowledged that their FOB needed to focus on continuous improvement activities to help streamline the process and examine gaps with tools and employee resources. Participants conducted a deep dive to determine the development of ideas for revenue growth, operational efficiency, and employee advancement. One participant offered that by performing these continuous activities, he determined whether more professional managers were needed to help prepare the business for the future.

> We are a lean environment. We've been lean for about 15 years. There are always varying degrees of lean manufacturing, but over the past two years, we've implemented, we call them a continuous improvement huddle. Typically, those leaders that I'm bringing up are really good at communication, at sharing, at the continuous improvement side of things. So, they're typically getting into those roles because they're better at it than their predecessor. You don't have to be over-engaged and the most active one in the CI huddles by any means.

Multiple participants educated their workforce regarding financials, helping to increase and improve their businesses. Spending money and informing the employees what they were doing also helped increase the perception of organizational health. When employees saw what transpired daily and had some input, they felt they were contributing in a positive way. One business owner reinforced this thought by stating, "I think that they see that we're using the money to grow the company. I think that shapes engagement in a big way. They know how they can contribute, and they can see what the company's doing with the money." When CEOs or owners communicate the financials to the employees, employees have a better understanding of when the numbers are good and when they are not.

Setting expectations throughout an FOB includes the message that there are no dumb ideas. When some participants allowed employees to express their ideas for others to hear or read, other employees learned from them, allowing all employees the opportunity to grow. One CEO commented, "So somebody puts it on there, and if it's a dumb idea, the supervisor does not get to take it off, because it hurts morale." Even when a concept is not going to be implemented, it nonetheless helps to create another idea from a different employee. This practical process helps the business increase revenue and facilitate ways to introduce operational efficiency.

In establishing continuous improvement, participants who afford employees the freedom to bring up issues and then allow them to research ways to resolve them create an environment of employee engagement. One participant declared, "The employees come up with ideas on how to make the job easier." When CEOs or owners ask employees for their ideas, employees' relationships are strengthened, bolstering the FOB's strategic development. When CEOs or owners have a strategic plan written down, they are more likely to work toward their goals and communicate the plan effectively to their employees and other stakeholders.

Your Time to Reflect:

- *Does your FOB have strategies and measures for growing the business?*
- *Does your business have strategies and measures for employee development? Do you review your bench strength to examine roles and responsibilities and look for both strengths and gaps in development?*
- *What does your FOB look like in 3-5 years?*
- *What are the strengths of your FOB? Weaknesses? Opportunities? Threats?*

CHAPTER 11

———— ❦ ————

SETTING EXPECTATIONS

The lessons I learned for this topic stem from my experience at Stop and Shop. As a young adult learning for the first time how to be a manager, I loved how the organization used both formal and informal ways of teaching standard work. No matter what store I was in as a trainee or manager, all the processes were done the same way. This was a direct result of the leadership and setting of expectations from the family who started, owned, and operated the food retail store. The leadership's expectations were passed down from generation to generation and highlighted formal on-the-job training. As a result, the family business never faded. When it comes to performance management, I think it is very important that leaders know how to set an expectation, get out of their offices and see what employees are doing, and then provide coaching feedback. When leaders set expectations and provide the leadership, training, and tools, they can expect that all employees, both family and nonfamily, will be working toward the same goals and objectives.

Setting expectations involves multiple actions across participant businesses. It includes providing information to some, gathering information for others, as well as understanding employees' readiness to the leadership changes. Setting the vision for the business establishes the expectation that employees and leadership are on the same page and united to reach a common business goal. Participants in my study who provided clear and calculated communication allowed their employees the opportunities for forward progress and mobility, and when employees were informed in a slow, thoughtful process, tensions and anxiety were eased, making the succession transition a nonevent. In setting expectations, multiple participants utilized assessments and surveys to gather information concerning employee awareness and to determine which expectations were being reached regarding the future changes of the FOB.

Growth opportunities are the paths of progressions provided by CEOs or owners to their employees to help the employees obtain new positions within the business as needed. In setting expectations, these new positions for growth opportunities benefit both the FOB and the employees. When participants provided paths of progressions, on varied levels, employees were able to move into the positions of need to help support the FOB's growth. With the proper training and diverse experiences, employees were ready to embrace the changes that occurred within the FOB. If the CEOs or owners plan to provide growth opportunities, and even have different locations for their businesses at some point in time, helping key potential family and nonfamily members gain experience is necessary.

When participants provided their employees with opportunities to grow, develop, participate, and add value, employees felt a sense of purpose. CEOs or owners who help employees feel a sense of purpose create a culture that is positive, contagious, and one that ultimately reflects the mission of the FOB. Numerous participants achieved this goal by outlining career paths and providing their employees with the education and feedback necessary for their own growth and development.

Learning and gaining experience are important skills to help one prepare to work within an FOB environment and to prepare one to be in a leadership role in the future. The company culture is such that employees feel comfortable about job security and safety at work. But if the company is small, with employee growth limited, every employee is not going to be able to move up and earn more. Yet, there are other ways in which employees could secure growth opportunities, and there are other factors that rank high for the employees to remain at the FOB, including flexible work hours, distance of travel, and vacation time, to name a few. One participant in the study shared this sentiment.

> As the owner and CEO of an FOB, I think there is a big difference in how employees see how far they can progress in the company. In my company, employees will only be able to grow so far in management. They will never get an opportunity to be an owner or the CEO in the FOB. Most of them will cap out at a management level. This is one of the drawbacks of being an FOB compared to a large nonfamily run operation that has many different levels and positions that employees can grow and develop into.

When participants were aware of their employees' desires for advancement or compensation in other areas of the FOB, they were then able to smoothly prepare for their transition. When asked to speak about his company's opportunities for growth, one owner added, "I think it is generally good. We're focusing on that more than ever, focusing on career paths, continuing education, quality, job enrichment." Awareness and opportunities are key elements in the succession planning process.

Some participants commented that some employees were perfectly content to continue as valued "soldiers" to the FOB, while others were frustrated because of the limited number of opportunities to advance. Establishing attainable expectations from the onset helps both the CEOs or owners of the FOB and the employees themselves evaluate the pressures being felt and courses that can be taken to target such concerns. One owner was aware of his employees' emotional dispositions and future desires.

> Obviously, my brother and I have both worked in the business for a number of years and we had, as a matter of fact, just worked hours and waited to be the senior managers and supervisors in the company. I think that

that dynamic has certainly contributed to this idea of things like, "I need to progress exceptionally quickly, or I need to have a change in high level positions at our relatively young ages," and that's been a challenge for us for sure.

In providing growth opportunities, CEOs or owners of the FOB work hard to keep employees motivated and see that the expectations set from the start are being met. Participants in my study encouraged employees to learn about the family business by providing educational opportunities like family business seminars or workshops. One owner professed, "As we grow as an FOB, we encourage career paths and getting our employees the education and feedback needed to give them plenty of opportunities to grow and develop." Another owner shared, "The employees in my FOB generally have a good feeling that if they have the skill set and the desire to grow and develop their career path, we will help them get there." Many participants recognized employees who were interested in continuing the mission of the FOB and were prepared to assume new leadership roles as needed.

Multiple participants understood that when employees who were identified as the future incumbents of the FOB started to understand what was needed to successfully assume that role, they spent countless hours learning the distinct aspects of the business. The children, or other nonfamily members, if necessary, were cognizant of each department, how each operated, and the amount of time needed to spend in each department to learn the varying aspects. They recognized the critical relationships already fostered with the customer and the vendors. In addition, the future incumbents knew how the current senior leaders felt about the past and present, and thus, future states of the FOB.

Various participants who disclosed to their employees that there were growth opportunities within the FOB created a work environment that supported the succession planning transition. Employees were more engaged and prepared to work through changes that would occur with the transition. For one participant, the succession planning transition became a nonevent when employees were guided, motivated, and excited to lead the FOB.

> It is nice to see that there are so many managers who have started at the bottom of the organization and worked their way up the chain to general managers. This is our informal development and growth plan for our FOB. We truly have seen a promotion from within our program. This also can help the younger employees just starting out to hear that managers and leaders all started in the same positions that they are in.

In providing growth opportunities, many participants agreed that they needed to develop a timeline of events, including when they wanted to transition from the business and then work backwards with the incumbent to prepare him or her, emotionally and professionally. These participants noted that this process could take a long time and should be treated with care and accountability. The FOB was more than just a business for the participants; it was a creation from their hearts and souls. As such, they needed to remember that the succession transition process should be managed in a similar fashion.

Shared information for a CEO or owner includes gathering data from diverse resources to provide detailed communication and statistics to employees, customers, and vendors. CEOs or owners utilize these instruments and techniques to better understand the pulse of the workforce and business landscape and to reinforce the expectations that are established for the succession planning transition. When the participants were thinking about transitioning out of their business and searching for a successor, they needed to share information with their employees, and they needed to collect information from them.

Various participants remarked that providing and collecting feedback could be a powerful tool to help maintain communication and build trust within the FOB. When the CEOs or owners had set expectations, they provided a vision for both the present and future of the business. The CEOs or owners were also establishing an environment where employees felt comfortable asking for information and were not threatened by this awareness, thus performing to their best abilities, the main objective of any participant.

In sharing information, numerous participants needed their employees' feedback, just like they sought information about products or news to and from their vendors. Obtaining feedback allows CEO or owners the means to communicate effectively. Frequent communication is important to limit interruptions with the flow of business, and for one participant, it showed employees that the CEO or owner was working with, and not against, them.

> They're threatened by change, so you have to really understand the dynamics of the organization and talk to the people who are really going to be affected by that change and get them to buy in, let them know they're not being threatened and the value of it. So whatever change you're making, they don't sabotage it through poor communication with that individual.

As soon as the participants investigated when the engagement levels changed with employees, they were able to get to the root causes of those changes and address those concerns. CEOs or owners who acknowledged their employees' apprehensions or fears created an environment which fostered trust and loyalty. One owner declared, "I think knowing the statistics of how many employees are actively disengaged at work compared to those who are actively engaged, having knowledge of those statistics is an eye opener." Without this information, it is difficult to determine if the business's expectations are being met, and it is difficult to move the FOB in a forward and progressive manner.

When sharing information, most participants mentioned that having transparent communication was one approach they used to establish and monitor the expectations they had established, and they maintained that this open communication eased the levels of the employees' anxiety towards the impending changes of the business. One CEO expressed, "Everybody in this world, I believe, does better with knowledge and with personal communication. If you talk to people personally and listen to them, they're going to be happier and do a better job and be more committed." Providing employee feedback, conducting quarterly meetings, having personal, one-on-one discussions with employees about the succession planning transition also leads to calmer, happier employees. This owner believed that employees who felt as though they were aware of what was occurring in their workforce added value to the FOB on multiple levels.

> I think having transparent communication with my leadership team can help them understand my role as CEO and my plans on staying in the position. My team understands the time it takes to put into a succession planning process. They also understand my expectation of starting to prepare for the next phase of the FOB.

Some participants stated that there needed to be a formalized communication process of how the succession planning transition would work. One participant asserted the importance of shared information and being transparent.

> Yes, I personally have communicated to my leadership team and others that I'm going to be the CEO and I'm going to retire in around the next five years. It takes a long time to plan these big, leadership shifts. I've learned from that, that I've got five years to get my succession planning under control, picking who's going to be the next CEO of the company, and who's going to take my roles from this day going forward and just being transparent about it with the people.

In setting expectations, participants who presented employees with honest feedback, whether through informal gatherings or formalized meetings, were building trust and emotionally preparing employees for changes that would occur throughout the succession planning transition. Formalized meetings with employees helped quell and eliminate unnecessary myths floating throughout the FOB concerning future leadership changes. Business owners need their employees to focus on the demands of the business and not waste time worrying or creating distractions about the steps in the transition process.

In providing emotional support, multiple participants invested in their FOBs by coaching their employees and outlining both the broader scope and details of their business. One owner stated, "I try to acknowledge that with them and give them more responsibility, and I try to have them mentored and coached, which are not always the same thing." Another participant shared, "We have our second-tier managers, and our first-tier manager is under us. They all have access to coaches, and they are mentored. They're trained on HR behavioral traits." Additionally, another owner stressed that coaching employees and teaching them to be self-aware helped secure the focus and process of the succession planning transition.

> Well, there is a two-fold answer to that. I'm talking about my two children and my niece. The coaching is integral. I try to spend time with each of them to give them a bigger view of the business and try to explain something to them, maybe a circumstance that I'm involved in or a situation to help show them how I'm handling it, to try to explain my philosophy of leadership. So, I think it's an investment of time as much as anything. But I think the coaching and the self-awareness are pretty important.

When CEOs or owners set an expectation, they can then monitor their actions and provide feedback to either seek improvement or offer praise to their employees.

Your Time to Reflect:

- *Is your leadership team trained to set goals and communicate?*
- *Do you have a formal communication plan that targets both company and personal developmental goals?*
- *Does your FOB have a formal performance feedback process? Is it implemented in a fair, firm, and consistent way?*
- *How do you hold your family and nonfamily employees accountable?*
- *How often do you get out of your office or go on the shop floor to observe and provide feedback?*

CHAPTER 12

❦

EMPLOYEE ENGAGEMENT

There is so much to be said about engagement and how to motivate employees to be at their best. The lessons I learned from my father and other leaders who mentored me over the years taught me the following about employee engagement. First, employee engagement starts with having a great leader who creates a work environment that generates growth and collaboration. We all need to remember that first businesses, especially FOBs, are an ecosystem and not a place where conflicts should exist. Second, the FOB is a community (with a heavy emphasis on the word community) of both family and nonfamily employees and not just a place to work. Third, I consider employees to be my peers, not my children, and I need to be a servant leader and not a boss. I really believe work should be a place of growth, and work should be fun and not a burden. Finally, motivation comes from leadership vision and transparent communication.

When I think of employee engagement, I see it as a positive, fulfilling, and motivating experience. Employee engagement also includes a willingness to work toward the successful achievement of work specifications and organizational goals (Albrecht, 2010; Macey et al., 2011). Researchers demonstrate that employee engagement is associated with a range of positive, individual, and organizational outcomes, and studies show that employee engagement is linked with increased employee well-being, increased job performance, cross-training performance, and reduced turnover (Crawford, LePine, & Rich, 2010; Halbeleben, J. 2010).

Perceptions of organizational health in both family and nonfamily employees have a direct impact on employee engagement and, thus, impact the business's ability to retain high potential employees. According to researchers, higher levels of employee engagement are associated with increased returns on assets, higher earnings per employee, higher performances, greater sales growth, and lower absenteeism (Albrecht et al., 2015). Throughout some of my exploration of this topic, I found that employee engagement is sometimes referred to as the harnessing of a business's employees to their work roles and responsibilities. This is important because employees express themselves physically and emotionally, as well as express themselves with their cognitive thoughts and emotions regarding their work output (Crawford et al., 2010). In my opinion, employee engagement within a business is established and results in a friendly environment where employees like each other and the work they perform. Employee engagement is linked to the significance of succession planning transition in that it includes finding the right employees with the right skill sets to be able to take over in key positions. By engaging the workforce, employees are more likely to want to grow, develop, and be considered part of the talent pool of possible candidates in the succession planning transition process.

Employee engagement changes over time because of the natural life cycle of a company, but it may be impacted by changing leadership within the business, including stages of succession planning. Employee engagement may also be influenced by the employer's perceptions of an employee's ability to grow within the business. If employees sense that they are treated well by leadership and given developmental opportunities to grow, then they would feel respected by the business.

Experts in the field do not have a well-established method to best describe, define, and measure employee engagement. What resonates with me is seeing employee engagement as a positive, fulfilling, work-related state of mind (Shaufeli et al., 2002). Employee engagement also includes a willingness to work toward the successful achievement of work specifications and organizational goals (Albrecht, 2002; Macey et al., 2011). Studies show that employee engagement is linked with increased employee well-being, increased job performance, increased cross-training performance, and reduced turnover (Crawford, LePine, & Rich, 2010; Halbeleben, J. 2010).

According to Pandita and Ray (2008), one of the most effective tools in ensuring that employees stay engaged and committed to their work is talent management. This sense of engagement or commitment toward their work ensures that these employees stay with the business in the long run. As the owners begin analyzing the costs associated with recruitment, selection, and the opportunity costs related to attrition, businesses concentrate their talent management efforts in the direction of retention (Pandita & Ray, 2008). As owners invest in developing their key employees, those employees would be ready when called upon to take on more responsibly as positions become vacant. This reinforces the significance of succession planning.

According to researchers, the effect of a Chief Executive Officer's leadership style has different effects on employees and their engagement level (Papalexandris & Galanki, 2009; Welch, 2011). Businesses aspire to have engaged employees, and leaders spend a tremendous amount of money and resources to measure and improve employee engagement. A leader's personality and how he or she acts in the workplace are as important as any benefit an employee might have acquired from the business (Howell, 2017).

Researchers argue that organizational leaders and the support they provide in setting a clear vision and specific goals might also directly influence employee engagement (Albrecht et al., 2015). If organizational leaders do not set a clear path forward for their employees, they might not have an employee who is capable and interested in being a successor in the business's key positions. Thus, this is significant to the development of employee engagement.

Employees who are engaged in their work are more energetic, are pleasant to be around, and have effective connections with their work (Macey & Schneider, 2008). According to researchers who conducted a study within healthcare and educational settings, employee engagement proves to be a significant predictor of desirable organizational outcomes such as employee retention, productivity, and employee development (Luthans & Peterson, 2002). Work engagement focuses on how psychological experiences of work shape the process of how employees view their work performance (Kahn, 1990). If employees have a good sense of their work performance, then they are more likely to grow and develop at work.

Engaged employees are believed to bring their full selves into their work roles and are cognitively attentive, emotionally vested, and physically energetic in their work environment (Crawford et al., 2010). When employees are engaged in their work, they are more likely to want to continuously improve themselves and the work that they do for the business. When family business owners or leaders communicate clearly what their organizational goals are to their employees, they help them perform to the best of their abilities.

Employees use social cues and information in the workplace not only concerning an employer's actions or inactions but also regarding their perceptions of these actions (Robinson, 1996). Consequently, if an owner of an FOB does not communicate effectively about his plans regarding succession planning, this could negatively impact an employee's perception of organizational health and engagement. Researchers show there is a strong association between human resource and organizational development practices and employee attitudes when engagement levels are high, and employees consider these human resource practices favorable to them (Farndale, Hope-Hailey, & Kelliher, 2011). Employees will respond in kind to the organization by giving their best.

Employee engagement is linked with a range of positive, individual, and business outcomes (Albrecht et al., 2018). Miller et al. (2016) explains that engaged employees have greater drive, longer longevity, and greater involvement in their perspective businesses. Researchers argue that employee engagement is presented as a critical component to a business to help leaders maintain their competitive advantage and financial profitability (Albrecht et al., 2015). The absence of employee engagement restricts a business's ability to promote from within, limiting the number of prospects considered for future succession transitions

(Bingham, 2008). Having a systematic process for succession planning helps the transition process run smoothly, ensuring future success for the business.

High performing employees demonstrate positive attitudes and employee engagement when human resource policy and practices send signals to employees about the business initiatives, the norms, and behaviors they display regarding employee development and growth (Malik & Singh, 2014). One can debate that employee engagement is directly and indirectly noticed through employee skill development of the job-related functions that an employee performs. More research is needed to fully understand how organizational factors such as human resource practices and organizational development relate to employee perceptions and performance (Albrecht et al., 2015).

Organizational culture includes the norms, values, and behaviors that employees share within the business. Organizational climate is the "personality" of a business as it relates to the attitudes and employee beliefs that could influence employees' collective behavior. If the behavior of the collective workforce, including both family and nonfamily members, is positive, and part of the organizational culture is developed and shows growth as part of the FOB's succession planning process, this would add value and would help to protect the business's market share and profitability.

Engaged employees create a company that has good organizational health. When employees contribute to their department, they have an impact on the profit margins. Throughout my study, many participants pointed out that each employee made a difference if he became engaged and performed the jobs that were assigned to him. These participants stated that as employees became more knowledgeable at work because of their tenure, they added value by introducing different ideas for growing the business and saving the company money. One owner discussed this impact.

> But just the net profits of the whole company are something that they can all impact. But they are impacted most significantly when they collaborate as

different departments because obviously it's a matter of marketing and sales and food production and event operations and just general administration to really see the margins be where they should be on the net.

In terms of business development, multiple participants commented that employee morale was a key component of organizational health and employee development. When CEOs or owners acknowledge their employees and the special times in their lives, both personally and professionally, these simple acts improve employee morale. One owner reinforced this by affirming, "I think sometimes simple little things, like also recognizing people's birthdays and anniversaries just takes the time to let people know that you thank them beyond the normal processes for their contributions to our success." Another pronounced, "I try to paint a fuller picture of people than just what you see at work." When participants took care of the personal needs of employees, this helped build loyalty to the business, and the employees performed better as a result.

CEOs or owners who have transparent communication with their workforce regarding succession planning for key positions support employees on numerous levels while also growing their business. When employees understand their roles and responsibilities and what positions are considered key, this develops an environment that promotes organizational health. Employees who feel comfortable with their superiors and engage in consistent, positive dialogue help the business grow and embrace the succession transition.

Many participants prepared for their futures by helping employees understand what was expected of them. One CEO announced, "I think that because of the family meetings and because the board was involved, I think that it was a very transparent process. And I think that future successions, wherever those may be, I think being transparent is important." Transparent communication begins the process of having all the right people in the right positions doing their jobs, adding value to the FOB, and promoting good organizational health.

Those participants who were active listeners and asked for guidance from employees helped drive the culture of the business. When incumbents are named, not everyone immediately trusts the judgment of the CEO or owner. Participants in the study noted that open communication helped ease these feelings and started the discussion process.

When an FOB has a systematic process of measuring engagement, the activities can be powerful in getting and keeping employees engaged at work. When leadership supports engagement activities, employees can feel empowered, motivated, and challenged.

Your Time to Reflect:

- *Do you have a diverse set of employee engagement activities? Examples for these activities would be recognizing employee tenure, providing opportunities for employees to socialize, providing engagement groups such as safety committees or continuous improvement committees.*
- *How does the FOB measure employee engagement?*
- *What do you look for to make sure your employees feel valued?*
- *What does the FOB do to motivate their employees?*

CHAPTER 13

FAMILY GOVERNANCE AND CONFLICT RESOLUTION

Family Retreat working on governance

For families that work together, it is important that family members set ground rules and a foundation of how they will communicate, participate, and quite frankly, how they will argue. There needs to be a set of rules that spell out roles, responsibilities, operating agreements, buying and selling agreements, and policies and procedures of how family members can come into the FOB so that there is a clear direction and understanding of such rules of engagement. Family members also need to know how to hold each other accountable and how often the family will meet during a given year. Furthermore, there needs to be an understanding of how some of the family's personal and professional matters can, and will, be handled.

In our family, we did not have very strict written rules, but there was the unwritten rule that if you worked in my father's business, you had to be the hardest working person at the store, you always took care of the customer, and you had to make sure your shirt and tie were cleaned and pressed. Also, my father was very adamant about what we could do outside of the business to offer entrepreneurial business services to our community. He felt that by having his last name, we needed to protect his legacy and the food it provided for us. My father worked long hours and never truly took time off from work. We did have family meals together on Tuesday and Sunday nights, and this was sacred to him and part of our family governance.

Family governance relates to the family structure and the importance of aligning both the business and the family's interests. Family governance is the development of family policies, procedures, and a code of conduct. According to my mentor, Stewart (2015), when an FOB works on its family governance, both the business and the family identifies the emotional issues before the emotions become the issue and negatively impact the succession planning transition.

Owners of FOBs need to not only deal with being a business owner, but they need to also manage being a leader of the family. Because of this, they may be frightened of losing their identity within the family structure that they have created (Stewart, 2015). Succession planning transition is a topic that faces resistance from business owners because of the changes in relationships within the family throughout the transition. Some of the changes that occur target the family system, including the role of the family members and their independence on the subsystems of the FOB and the owner.

FOBs could fail for many reasons, including family conflicts over money, poor management by family members who are not qualified, and infighting when determining who has the right to take over the business (Casper, Dia, & Elstrodt, 2010). According to Carlock and Ward (2001), from time to time, families may experience relationship problems, including the children's desire to differentiate themselves from their parents, marital discord, or ownership dispersion among family members as being central to every family (Eddleston & Kellermanns, 2007). A study was conducted with 392 Austrian family businesses that examined how family climate could impact family business performance, and the results of this study demonstrated the negative effects of relationships on FOBs' satisfaction and performance (Nosé, Korunka, Frank, & Danes, 2017). This is parallel to my research study about how perceptions of engagement and organizational health impact the succession planning process.

According to Nietzche (1997), in FOB successions, there may be a dilemma of the burden of history and the battle for the future among the generations of fathers and sons. As the younger generation seeks to embrace its own visions for the future of the business, conflicts may arise with older generation employees who want to pass on what they have developed and see it continue to grow (Eddleston & Kellemanns, 2007). This presents challenges as next-generation employees coming into their own may want to act independently and not be burdened with the responsibilities of the business.

Clearly, family relationships may be very problematic for families working within FOBs. However, when a succession planning transition is established, this helps family members who are working in lower levels learn how to progress into key positions within the business. Having a succession planning transition in place also encourages family members who are not currently involved in the FOB to learn about the business and determine what they need to do to become an integral part of the business.

When the leadership of a family and the FOB develop a family council, this can give family members a voice and can help them stay engaged within the ownership of the FOB. When CEOs or owners allow healthy debates, this can also help bring about change. However, good conflict resolution skills are needed so employees do not feel they are stuck because of a conflict.

Your Time to Reflect:

- *What role does each family member have within the FOB?*
- *How often does the family meet to discuss business, ownership, and the family?*
- *What does good family governance look like for your family?*
- *What formal and informal committees need to be in place in order to have family structure?*
- *Do you have a sibling or family code of conduct?*
- *Do you provide conflict resolution tools among family, senior leaders, and employees?*

CHAPTER 14

SENIOR LEADERSHIP, TALENT DEVELOPMENT, AND HIGH POTENTIAL EMPLOYEES

My father taught me that I should always be looking out for people who are talented and have the skills and visions that I possess in order to help me grow. This is a "value" proposition; I want to learn from the people with whom I work, and I want them to learn from me. My father also helped me to understand the importance of having a strong, dedicated, superhero-like work ethic and to always be proactive. He impressed upon us all that if you learn from your mistakes, you will grow as a result. From these lessons, I always strive to be the best I can be. So, when I think of high potential employees, these are individuals who are not afraid to take a chance and stretch themselves, knowing that they will fail in order to succeed.

Talent within a company must be identified, segmented, nurtured, and placed into challenging positions, not only to grow, but to also help the business become more competitive (Boudreau & Ramstad, 2005). Researchers show that leaders are capable of effectively identifying and encouraging junior employees with strong leadership potential to enter the leadership pipeline (Myung et al., 2011). High potential employees are thought of as those individuals whose current and future contributions and efforts are key to the success of a business.

Succession planning within FOBs is thought of as the process of identifying high potential employees who can run a business in the years to come. If leaders of family businesses are unable to find the right fit to lead their workforce, they may need to sell the business or liquidate the assets, impacting the company, the employees, and the family. Thus, CEOs or owners of FOBs need to think carefully when choosing a successor who can take over and preserve the business.

A leadership development plan helps develop clear and specific goals for employee development for both family and nonfamily members. A good FOB should engage all its employees to look at their strengths and weaknesses to create a developmental plan to address any skill gaps. In addition, a good leadership development plan should provide structured feedback and a coaching process to help both the owner and its employees feel comfortable understanding each other's roles and responsibilities. A good leadership development plan utilizes developmental programs that teach principles of coaching and mentoring to help the individuals reach their full potential as leaders.

Many family businesses are not able to manage successful successions to the next generation due to poor successor nurturing (Samei & Feyzbakhsh, 2016). Successor nurturing is the process of working and mentoring employees to help them learn the critical skills needed to perform as leaders. Leaders need to possess the right set of competencies to be able to mentor and train employees to be successful. When an incumbent feels he or she is getting the training and mentoring needed, he or she feels more comfortable accepting more responsibility. Thus, when an owner finds a successor and starts training that individual and transferring knowledge through nurturing and mentoring, the owner also feels more comfortable and is more willing to start thinking about retiring.

A major struggle for FOBs is finding the right successor to take over the business (Sharma, 2004). Some businesses struggle with succession planning and talent management because leadership feels they do not have the talent pool within their ranks and files and fails to find the talent outside. Many FOB owners only look at their family as candidates to take over the business, but this could be an issue because of the limited amount of talent within the family to do so. Not having family members who are competent to take over adds a great deal of stress and frustration to both the employees and the owner (deVires, 1993).

One of the many problems associated with FOBs is selecting the right person to lead the business for the next generation (deVires, 1993). If a family has a plan to transition the company to another family member, it is imperative that that individual is capable and competent to lead the workforce. If a company does not have family members who have the skills to take over the company, it could cause problems, including having key nonfamily members who feel they do not have a career path and are excluded from senior positions (Gallo & Vilaseca, 1998). Other employees may feel they are being overlooked, and this could cause turnover with key employees who have a significant role in the success of the company, creating a new set of problems. The FOB cannot afford to lose key employees who help add to the profit of the business and help sustain the business for future generations.

Another challenge faced by owners is to hire and retain talented nonfamily members who are motivated to take on supervisory responsibilities (Young, Peng, Ahlstrom, Bruton, & Jiang, 2008). However, FOB owners enjoy their privacy and prefer to stay within their family circle and trusted advisors, and they view nonfamily managers as people who do not work as hard or are as dedicated to the business as family members are (Chua et al., 2003). Some FOB owners do not consider nonfamily members as part of their succession transition and do not see the value of training them, causing problems with the FOB surviving past the first generation (Ibrahim et al., 2003). Succession planning transition is a concern regarding the survival of FOBs of all varied sizes in population and revenue, not only for the business, but also for those who rely on the company for their livelihood (Sambrook, 2005). However, FOBs are often required to rely on nonfamily employees in both lower and upper-level positions, though nonfamily employees bring a unique set of challenges to FOBs.

According to Carsrud (2006), it is difficult to secure nonfamily employees' commitment and cooperation working for FOBs because they do not perceive that the owners support them, and they are not considered full-fledged and valued members of the FOB. Nonfamily members working for FOBs are obliged to deal with and adjust to the owner of the company and his or her set of expectations, and difficulty with this transition leads to morale and productivity issues. Additionally, when an owner needs to delegate some decision-making authority to a nonfamily member, and that nonfamily member feels he is not compensated for the work he is doing, issues arise such as loss of productivity, a sense of disloyalty to the business, and turnover (Jensen & Meckling, 1976). Nonfamily members want a sense of ownership for the work that they produce, and they want to be properly compensated for the contributions they make to the business (Schulze, Lubatkin, Dino, & Buchholtz, 2001).

Talent within a company needs to be identified, segmented, nurtured, and placed into challenging positions, not only to grow, but to also help the business become more competitive (Boudreau & Ramstad, 2005). Researchers show that leaders are capable of effectively identifying and encouraging junior employees with strong leadership potential to enter the leadership pipeline (Myung et al., 2011). Talent identification has an impact on how employees identify with their employer (Björkman, Ehrnrooth, Mäkelä, Smale, & Sumelius, 2013), and when businesses perceive that they have found and developed talent, their employees are more committed toward their employer (Morrison & Robinson, 1997; Zhao, Wayne, Glibkowski, & Bravo, 2007).

Talent identification is an overly critical part of the succession planning transition. When family-owned leaders seek out high potential employees, they are creating a pipeline of employees to take on leadership positions and responsibilities within the business. Regarding talent identification, if employees know that they have a path of progression, a business could look to promote talented employees who are both family and nonfamily members, giving them a sense that the business is thriving and operating in a way that is promoting organizational health.

When owners do not have the talent within their family to take over the business, they must look at nonfamily members as options, and often, FOBs rely on nonfamily members for the businesses to survive (Chua et al., 2003). Owners need to find key managers in their businesses who they can trust and who share the same values as they do to give up some control and allow nonfamily members to run their business. This relationship of trust between owners and all employees, including family and nonfamily employees, is one that must be developed and nurtured over time.

Owners must think strategically about how they develop and manage their talent (Sale, 1987). Talent management relates to how businesses reward and recognize their exceptionally talented employees. However, there is a lack of clarity concerning the definition of talent management and how it is used with succession planning transition (Lewis & Heckman, 2006).

According to researchers, there is a set of human resource practices within a FOB that are to be followed to help predict and support the flow of human capital based on the family and nonfamily employees' skills, knowledge, and ability (Lewis & Heckman, 2006). Talent management is used to reward employees who are identified as high potential employees, those who succeed in their current positions and keep growing and assuming more responsibility within a business. Managing talent within a business is important because if leaders seek talent outside the business, internal talent might see this as a threat, undermining teamwork and increasing turnover (Pfeffer, 2001).

When owners use coaching and mentoring, they are developing the next generation of leaders. Coaching is incredibly significant and relevant to the succession planning transition to help give successors in key positions opportunities to seek guidance and develop the expertise to step in when needed by the business. If owners utilize coaching as a continuous learning tool, they can be more prepared to make succession decisions in a timelier fashion and stay within the business when a position needs to be filled. Also, if incumbents use coaching, they are teaching coaching skills to the next generation to help develop their future successors.

If owners of FOBs have capable family members in the right positions, they would stay competitive in the market and have a qualified bench that is ready and willing to take over if, and when, they need to transition. If owners have their children and other family members working for them, the owners need to make sure they have the proper tools in place to teach the skills and knowledge the family members would need to contribute to the business. Thus, owners who invest in developing their family members help a succession process because it allows for the development of an individualized plan to enhance the family members' skills and talents which could be used to strengthen the FOB. If family members have specific roles and responsibilities within the FOB, this reduces any conflicts or communication breakdown that interferes with the succession transition of who is the next in line to assume leadership positions.

Developing nonfamily employees is particularly important to the succession planning transition because the family may have only a limited number of family members who work for the business. Owners develop nonfamily members because they have family working within the company but do not have the leadership characteristics to run the business. Owners of FOBs who recognize that nonfamily members are key to the survival of their business impact the financial bottom line of the profit and loss statement, while looking at some of these employees in key positions to be part of the succession process and keeping the continuity of the FOB when they experience turnover with some key leadership positions.

Taking time to hire family and nonfamily members properly is one of the most important decisions and responsibilities an owner makes. An owner needs to learn how to be a coaching manager/leader and spend quality time developing any employee he sees as a successor. A coaching manager is someone who uses coaching to develop talent to obtain the results he needs (Hunt & Weintraub, 2016). Leadership needs to understand the importance of providing training and development to help support the succession planning transition with the correct leadership competencies.

Researchers report that as businesses compete in a more global marketplace, leaders need to think about their businesses and the shortage of potential leaders among their current workforce and the need to develop the training for those employees who have the proper skills, knowledge, and ability to be considered for leadership positions

(Copland, 2001). When leaders use coaching and skill development to share their experiences with the successor, positive results occur, including the identification of the competencies needed for the employees to develop the skills, knowledge, and capabilities to achieve the leadership performance (Samei & Feyzbakhsh, 2016). Additionally, sharing feedback during coaching significantly helps in improving the successor's managerial and technical knowledge and skills to take over as the leader (Samei & Feyzbakhsh, 2016). Thus, it is evident that leaders must have the critical skill set of being able to train and develop their next generation (Adedayo, Olanipekun, & Ojo, 2016).

When CEOs or owners have a list of high potential employees, they can start grooming them and getting them ready to be backfills for the succession planning process. With a list of high potential employees, the CEO or owner looks at gaps and the needs of the business and focuses his or her energy and time on that list of high potential employees. According to Ozclik (2015), one of the biggest mistakes with succession planning transition is not internally engaging the workforce. Researchers found that high performing employees demonstrate positive attitudes and employee engagement when human resource policy and practices send signals to employees about the business initiatives, the norms, and behaviors they displayed regarding employee development and growth (Malik & Singh, 2014). Researchers show that leaders are capable of effectively identifying and encouraging junior employees with strong leadership potential to enter the leadership pipeline (Myung et al., 2011).

When CEOs or owners develop their senior leadership team, it reduces resistance for a succession plan for both the CEO or owner and any of the key leadership positions. If an FOB does not have family members who have the skills to take over the company, it causes problems, including having key nonfamily members who feel they do not have a career path and are excluded from senior positions (Gallo & Vilaseca, 1998). Researchers state that successors place weight on the fact that key nonfamily members who work for the FOBs need to be part of the succession planning transitions for the succession planning process and transition of power to be successful from the incumbent to the successor (Ensley & Pearson, 2005). Studies reveal that as FOBs grow, they need to be dependent upon nonfamily managers because the owners only have a limited number of family members willing and capable to be involved in management and leadership positions (Chua et al., 2003).

Your Time to Reflect:

- *Do you have a process of identifying high potential employees and a method to track their performance?*
- *How do you communicate your succession plan process and timing with your senior leadership team?*
- *What does the succession plan for each member of your senior leadership team look like?*
- *Do you provide stretch assignments?*
- *Do you have individual developmental plans for both family and nonfamily employees who show potential?*

CHAPTER 15

CLARITY OF ROLES AND RESPONSIBILITIES

As an Industrial/Organizational Business Psychologist and being an HR professional working with my internal clients, I always seek clarity to better understand the "what", "why", and "how" people do their work. I feel that if employees understand how they make an impact both personally and professionally on the business and get the training and tools to do the work, they will perform to the best of their abilities. If family and nonfamily members say it is not my role or in my job description, this can be an issue for continuous improvement. It also becomes an issue with sustaining and protecting the owner's legacy, and this can damage a succession planning process.

As stated in the previous chapter, studies show that as FOBs grow, owners need to be dependent upon nonfamily managers because they may only have a limited number of family members willing and capable to be involved in management and leadership positions (Chua, Chrisman, & Sharma, 2003). Accordingly, as FOBs grow, owners often need to depend on nonfamily managers who have the experience and expertise to run the daily operations of the business (Chua et al., 2003). Studies show that recruitment of nonfamily members is important, not only for leadership levels, but also for the rank-and-file positions that lead into positions of management (Sambrook, 2005). Thus, FOBs need to attract the best talent to help meet the needs of the business. To do so, owners need to start early, establish good human resource practices, and develop career ladders for their nonfamily members to help maintain their workforce during times of growth (Storey & Sission, 1993).

Owners of FOBs must understand and recognize when they reach a point where they cannot manage alone, they need others who are not family members to help in specific positions such as finance, sales, operations, and human resources to help with the future transfer of power when the owner is ready for the succession (Sambrook, 2005). Nonfamily members who demonstrate that they are committed to the FOB and could develop a strong relationship with their owners enhance the workplace culture. When nonfamily members display a good understanding of the business's mission, vision, values, and goals and incorporate them in their work, they also enhance the trust level with the owners. As the relationships continue to grow with owners and nonfamily members, this presents opportunities for growth and development for nonfamily members.

If owners start considering nonfamily members to undertake key positions within the business, this strengthens the commitment and loyalty that the nonfamily members have to the FOB. However, giving up control and allowing nonfamily managers to control the business is not an easy transition for family owners because they feel they may lose the organizational culture they have developed, creating interfamily conflict (Lester & Cannella, 2006). Potential conflict issues need to be examined, and the business must address these issues through conflict resolution, relationship building among their Board of Directors, professionalization of owners' management style, and overall decision making by the owners (Chua et al., 2003). As owners of FOBs begin to feel comfortable with their own learning and development with nonfamily members, they become more comfortable transferring their knowledge to others within their business, even if they are nonfamily members (Gary & Lawless, 2000).

Leadership succession is critical to ensure the transfer of knowledge and responsibility for the ongoing management of the business from members of the senior family to the junior family members (Blumentrit, Matthews, & Marchisio, 2013). The owner must determine if the successor appointed is ready to lead the business. Researchers show that incumbents vary in the extent of readiness to take over leadership, which is known as being succession ready or non-succession ready (Marler et al., 2017). According to Cabrera-Suárez (2005), change is an inherent part of the succession transition, and leaders need to be willing to let go of their leadership responsibilities to have a successful transfer of power.

It is necessary for owners to have a plan in place and be able to have the family members be willing and capable to help with the responsibility of taking over the business. Family members who are interested in taking over the business need to have the right personality traits and display the right behaviors such as learning new responsibilities and making independent decisions (Cabrera-Suárez, 2005; Handler, 1994). Staffing issues within businesses are associated with issues around succession as businesses lack talent and the right attributes that are needed to assume leadership roles within the FOBs (McDonald, 2008). It is essential for the owner and the senior family member to be able to mentor and develop the identified younger family member or members to help him or her develop the skills needed to be successful in taking over the business (Marler et al., 2017). It is also important for the successors to have a good relationship with key, nonfamily members to help retain and attract new, nonfamily members (Chua et al., 2003).

Succession planning takes time, and there is a solid amount of planning that needs to take place to help the owner of the family transfer control of his business to the successor. Lansberg (1988) states that incumbents have a great deal of power in the succession transition and can facilitate the process or slow it down by interfering with it. According to Marler et al., (2017), role transitions in succession planning have a long-lasting impact on individuals and businesses. It is important for the FOB owner to select the right person to lead the company to the next generation, and that individual must possess the skills and knowledge to keep the business going. Once a successor is selected, it is important that the incumbent and the successor develop a vision, or strategic plan, for the business after the succession, to define the roles and responsibilities of the departing incumbent and to communicate the succession decision to all key stakeholders, including the nonfamily members who may have been considered.

Professional management, or professionalization, is the process through which FOBs formalize internal processes and hire nonfamily managers to run the businesses (Stewart & Hitt, 2012). According to researchers, professionalization has five major components that could help an FOB develop systems to help transition from one generation to the next. They include introduction to financial control systems, nonfamily involvement in governance systems, human resource systems, decentralization of authority, and development of a formal, top-level leadership meeting process (Dekker, Lybaert, Stijvers, Depaire, & Mercken, 2013).

Professionalization supports the need for formal processes and human resources to allow for succession planning to efficiently take place. For example, if the owner cannot find an internal candidate to take over as the successor, then finding the right external candidate would be critical if the owner wants to maintain the business moving forward. Also, the owners may want to make an investment in infrastructure, like technology and/or additional formal human resource policies and procedures to help the external leader develop the tools he or she needs to run the business. This could also help the next generation become prepared to take over the business if they are too young or do not have the skills yet to take over from the older generation.

Role transitions for the owners, executives, and successors are quite different depending on the proactive personality of each person (Parker, 1988). A proactive personality is the behavior of displaying initiative by changing the workplace in a positive, constructive way (Seibert, Kraimer, & Crant, 2001). Researchers state that proactive personalities are critical to the organizational change regarding succession planning transition (Bateman & Crant, 1993). It is essential for owners and leaders to have the right mindset for the succession transition to be successful, and they need to also find the most qualified employees who display a positive mindset. Conducting a job analysis and job description for an outgoing owner, CEO, or key position is important to determine if there is a 1-for-1 replacement or if additional resources are needed.

Your Time to Reflect:

- *Do you have a detailed job analysis and descriptions that outline key roles and responsibilities for all critical positions that might need a succession plan?*
- *What are the key titles and roles for your FOB?*
- *What are the key responsibilities for both family and nonfamily employees?*
- *Do you have backup employees cross-trained to play an interim role if needed?*

CHAPTER 16

CONCLUSION

It is especially important for an organization to think through and communicate its strategic management process to ensure all employees understand their roles in creating and maintaining the business's competitive advantage in the marketplace. It is also particularly important that organizations take their time to develop their overall vision, goals, and values. Once the organization has developed its strategic management process, leaders can then communicate to their shareholders, vendors, suppliers, and external customers methods they will use to maintain their difference, and thus advantage, among competitors. Part of this all-important step for a leader is to select his or her successor to make sure that the knowledge transfer has taken effect and that the outgoing and the incoming CEO or owner has a solid handle of the FOB's performance.

CEOs and business owners need to understand the value of money and acknowledge and plan how they want to utilize it to grow the business. If the business wants to expand its facilities, purchase new equipment, invest in employee development, add staff, or simply add new product lines to be more competitive, it will need to make an investment. Understanding the ratios and the value of the return on the investment are critical skills to making important decisions that will impact the development of the business. The same thinking needs to be used regarding succession planning to maintain the FOB's competitive advantage.

As I stated earlier in the book, family-owned businesses play a key role in the global economy. According to Whitehouse (2010), 36 million baby-boomer Americans are turning 65 over the next decade and another 45 million in the next 20 years after that. Family business succession is timely and important. It can be difficult to find the right fit in any organization, but it can be even more difficult when the owner must think about his own children and determine if they are capable of running the company after he or she retires. If FOB owners do not have the conversation regarding their succession, they are putting the company and the family at jeopardy.

The purpose of my succession study was to explore practices that CEOs or owners in FOBs used in their succession planning transitions. As I detailed in each chapter, one of the primary outcomes was the development of an assessment to assist practitioners, scholars, and other CEOs or owners with identifying the level of preparedness for succession planning transitions. Another significant finding from my research study was that the CEOs or owners needed to be respectful of their past and mindful of the present to be best prepared for the future. As I reflect on this journey to better understand the CEOs' or owners' perceptions and practices of how they perceive employee engagement and the organizational health of the succession planning transition, it became apparent that one size does not fit all, and utilizing an assessment or deep dive can help formulate a plan that targets the needs of each unique family-owned business.

It is my wish that owners of family businesses, their families, C-Suite executives, and any and all advisors understand the Kerzner STAMP and spend the quality time to prepare themselves for the succession planning journey. I wrote this book to help CEOs/owners pass on their legacy and the lessons they learned through the years. I am confident my research and stories can also help owners reduce their resistance and encourage them to hire nonfamily professionals to carry on the legacy for the family until the next generation is ready. Furthermore, this book can help owners with a liquidity event like my father experienced if that is the path they are choosing.

I sincerely hope business owners consider using STAMP to fit their unique family and business needs. By having a plan in place, owners can remove the emotions and work off facts and data of the past and present to then be best prepared for the future. If any reader would like to further this discussion, I am thrilled to do so. I can be reached at matthew.necfbe@gmail.com.

Quality time with my family in Hawaii before
defending my research dissertation

REFERENCES

Adedayo, O. S., Olanipekun, O. J., & Ojo, O. (2016). Planning for succession and firm's sustainability: Evidence from family owned businesses in Lagos and Ogun States, Nigeria. *Issues in Business Management and Economics*, 4(6), 63-69.

Ahlers, O., Hack, A., & Kellermanns, F. W. (2014). "Stepping into the buyers' shoes": Looking at the value of family firms through the eyes of private equity investors. *Journal of Family Business Strategy*, 5(4), 384-396.

Albrecht, S.L. (Ed.). (2010). *Handbook of employee engagement: Perspectives, issues, research and practice*. Glos, England: Edward Elgar.

Albrecht, S. L., Bakker, A. B., Gruman, J. A., Macey, W. H., & Saks, A. M. (2015). Employee engagement, human resource management practices and competitive advantage: An integrated approach. *Journal of Organizational Effectiveness: People and Performance*, 2(1), 7-35.

Albrecht, S., Breidahl, E., & Marty, A. (2018). Organizational resources, organizational engagement climate, and employee engagement. *Career Development International*, 23(1), 67-85.

Aloulou, W. J. (2018). Examining entrepreneurial orientation's dimensions–performance relationship in Saudi family businesses: Contingency role of family involvement in management. *Journal of Family Business Management*, 8(2), 126-145.

Anderson, M. L. (2003). Embodied cognition: A field guide. *Artificial Intelligence*, 149(1), 91-130.

Ashkanasy, N. M. (2003). Emotions in organizations: A multi-level perspective. In F. Dansereau, & F. J. Yammarino (Eds.), *Research in multi-level issues, Vol. 2.* (pp. 9–54). Oxford, UK: Elsevier Science.

Ayres, G. R. (1990). Rough family justice: Equity in family business succession planning. *Family Business Review, 3*(1), 3-22.

Banschick, M. (2012). The high failure rate of second and third marriages. *Psychology Today, 6.*

Barach, J. A., Gantisky, J., Ourson, J. A., & Doochin, B. A. (1988). Entry of the next generation: Strategic challenge for family business. *Journal of Small Business Management, 3,* 12.

Baron, A., & Armstrong, M. (2007). *Human capital management: achieving added value through people.* London, UK: Kogan Page Publishers.

Barnett, T., & Kellermanns, F. W. (2006). Are we family and are we treated as family? Nonfamily employees' perceptions of justice in the family firm. *Entrepreneurship Theory and Practice, 30*(6), 837-854.

Bateman, T. S., & Crant, J. M. (1993). The proactive component of organizational behavior: A measure and correlates. *Journal of Organizational Behavior, 14*(2), 103-118.

Bazeley, P. (2009). Analyzing mixed methods data. *Mixed methods research for nursing and the health sciences, 2,* 84-118.

Bingham, T. (2008). The talent factor. *Public Manager, 37*(3), 80.

Björkman, I., Ehrnrooth, M., Mäkelä, K., Smale, A., & Sumelius, J. (2013). Talent or not? Employee reactions to talent identification. *Human Resource Management, 52*(2), 195-214.

Blocknick, S. (1984). The case of the reluctant heirs. *Forbes, 134*(2), 180.

Blumentritt, T., T. Matthews, and G. Marchisio. (2013). Game theory and family business succesion. *Family Buinsess Review, 26*(1), 51-67.

Boudreau, J. W., & Ramstad, P. M. (2005). Talentship, talent segmentation, and sustainability: A new HR decision science paradigm for a new strategy definition. *Human Resource Management, 44*(2), 129-136.

Bozer, G., Levin, L., & Santora, J. C. (2017). Succession in family business: Multi-source perspectives. *Journal of Small Business and Enterprise Development, 24*(4), 753-774.

Breton-Miller, I. L., Miller, D., & Steier, L. P. (2004). Toward an integrative model of effective FOB succession. *Entrepreneurship Theory and Practice, 28*(4), 305-328.

Brockhaus, R. H. (2004). Family business succession: Suggestions for future research. *Family Business Review, 17*(2), 165-177.

Butler, K., & Roche-Tarry, D. E. (2002). Succession planning: Putting an organization's knowledge to work. *Nature Biotechnology, 20*(2), 201-202.

Byham, W. C. (2002). A new look at succession management. *Ivey Business Journal, 66*(5), 10-12.

Cabrera-Suárez, K. (2005). Leadership transfer and the successor's development in the family firm. *The Leadership Quarterly, 16*(1), 71-96.

Cabrera-Suárez, K., De Saá-Pérez, P., & García-Almeida, D. (2001). The succession process from a resource-and knowledge-based view of the family firm. *Family Business Review, 14*(1), 37-46.

Carlock, R., & Ward, J. (2001). *Strategic planning for the family business: Parallel planning to unify the family and business.* Houndsmill, NY: Palgrave.

Carsrud, A. L. (2006). Commentary: "Are we family and are we treated as family? Nonfamily employees' perceptions of justice in the family firm": It all depends on perceptions of family, fairness, equity, and justice. *Entrepreneurship Theory and Practice, 30*(6), 855-860.

Carsrud, A., Perez, S. E. and Sachs, R. (1996). Exploring a classification scheme for closely-held businesses: getting to workable definitions of family firms. In *Proceedings of the world conference of the family business network,* Edinburgh, Scotland.

Casper, C., Dias, A. K., & Elstrodt, H. P. (2010). The five attributes of enduring family businesses. *McKinsey Quarterly, 1,* 1-10.

Caspersz, D., & Thomas, J. (2015). Developing positivity in family business leaders. *Family Business Review, 28*(1), 60-75.

Chrisman, J. J., Chua, J. H., Sharma, P., & Yoder, T. R. (2009). Guiding family businesses through the succession process. *The CPA Journal, 79*(6), 48.

Christension, C. (1953) *Management succession in small and growing enterprises*. Boston, MA: Division of Research, Harvard Business School.

Chua, J. H., Chrisman, J. J., & Sharma, P. (2003). Defining the family business by behavior. *Entrepreneurship Theory and Practice, 23*(4), 19-39.

Church, A. H., Shull, A. C., & Burke, W. W. (2018). Organization development and talent management: Divergent sides of the same values equation. In *Enacting values-based change* (pp. 265-294). Cham, Switzerland: Palgrave Macmillan.

Collins, O. F., Moore, D. G., & Unwalla, D. (1964). The enterprising man and the business executive. *MSU Business Topics, 12*(1), 19-34.

Copland, M. A. (2001). The myth of the superprincipal. *Phi Delta Kappan, 82*(7), 528-533.

Crawford, E. R., LePine, J. A., & Rich, B. L., & Halbeleben, J. (2010). Linking job demands and resources to employee engagement and burnout: A theoretical extension and meta-analytic test. *Journal of Applied Psychology, 95*(5), 834.

Daspit, J. J., Chrisman, J. J., Sharma, P., Pearson, A. W., & Long, R. G. (2017). A strategic management perspective of the family firm: Past trends, new insights, and future directions. *Journal of Managerial Issues, 29*(1), 6-29.

Davis, W. D., Dibrell, C., Craig, J. B., & Green, J. (2013). The effects of goal orientation and client feedback on the adaptive behaviors of family enterprise advisors. *Family Business Review, 26*(3), 215-234.

Dekker, J. C., Lybaert, N., Steijvers, T., Depaire, B., & Mercken, R. (2013). Family firm types based on the professionalization construct: Exploratory research. *Family Business Review, 26*(1), 81-99.

De Massis, A., Chua, J. H., & Chrisman, J. J. (2008). Factors preventing intra-family succession. *Family Business Review, 21*(2), 183-199.

De Massis, A., Sieger, P., Chua, J. H., & Vismara, S. (2016). Incumbents' attitude toward intrafamily succession: An investigation of its antecedents. *Family Business Review, 29*(3), 278-300.

DeSmet, P. M., & Pohlmeyer, A. E. (2013). Positive design: An introduction to design for subjective well-being. *International Journal of Design, 7*(3), 5-19.

de Vries, M. F. K. (1993). The dynamics of family-controlled firms: The good and the bad news. *Organizational Dynamics, 21*(3), 59-71.

Eddleston, K. A., & Kellermanns, F. W. (2007). Destructive and productive family relationships: A stewardship theory perspective. *Journal of Business Venturing, 22*(4), 545-565.

Ensley, M. D., & Pearson, A. W. (2005). An exploratory comparison of the behavioral dynamics of top management teams in family and nonfamily new ventures: Cohesion, conflict, potency, and consensus. *Entrepreneurship Theory and Practice, 29*(3), 267-284.

Epstein, G. (2010). Replacements ease labor pain. *Barron's, 90*(4). Retrieved from https://www.barrons.com/articles/ SB126421165590533459?tesla=y

Family business succession planning white paper. (2016). *Family Business Institute Inc.* Retrieved from https://www.familybusinessinstitute. com/wp-content/uploads/ 2019/01/Family-Business-Succession-Planning-White-Paper.pdf

Family Owned Statistics (2016, September 08). *Statistic Brain Research Institute.* Retrieved from http://www.statisticbrain.com/ Family-Owned-buisness-statistics/

Farndale, E., Hope-Hailey, V., & Kelliher, C. (2011). High commitment performance management: The roles of justice and trust. *Personnel Review, 40*(1), 5-23.

Fineman, S. (2000). Emotional arenas revisited. In S. Fineman (Ed.), *Emotion in organizations,* (pp. 1-24). Thousand Oaks, CA: Sage Publications.

Frank, H., Kessler, A., Rusch, T., Suess-Reyes, J., & Weismeier-Sammer, D. (2017). Capturing the families of family businesses: Development of the family influence familiness scale (FIFS). *Entrepreneurship Theory and Practice, 41*(5), 709-742.

Gallo, M. A., & Vilaseca, A. (1998). A financial perspective on structure, conduct, and performance in the family firm: An empirical study. *Family Business Review, 11*(1), 35-47.

Gary, C., & Lawless, N. (2000). Innovations in the distance development of SME management skills. *European Journal of Open, Distance and E-Learning, 3*(2), 1-8.

Gersick, K. E., Davis, J. A., Hampton, M. M., & Lansberg, I. (1997). *Empresas familiares: generación a generación.* México: McGraw-Hill.

Getz, D., & Carlsen, J. (2000). Characteristics and goals of family and owner-operated businesses in the rural tourism and hospitality sectors. *Tourism Management, 21*(6), 547-560.

Grandey, A. A. (2000). Emotional regulation in the workplace: A new way to conceptualize emotional labor. *Journal of Occupational Health Psychology, 5*(1), 95.

Greenberg, J., & Cropanzano, R. (1993). The social side of fairness: Interpersonal and informational classes of organizational justice. In *Justice in the workplace: Approaching fairness in human resource management.* Hillsdale, NJ: Lawrence Erlbaum Associates.

Handler, W. C. (1990). Succession in family firms: A mutual role adjustment between entrepreneur and next-generation family members. *Entrepreneurship Theory and Practice, 15*(1), 37-52.

Handler, W. C. (1994). Succession in family business: A review of the research. *Family Business Review, 7*(2), 133-157.

Handler, W. C., & Kram, K. E. (1988). Succession in family firms: The problem of resistance. *Family Business Review, 1*(4), 361-381.

Härtel, C. E., & Hsu, A. C. (2002). *Managing emotions in the workplace.* Armonk, NY: ME Sharpe.

Hjorth, D., & Dawson, A. (2016). The burden of history in the family business organization. *Organization Studies, 37*(8), 1089-1111.

Holsapple, C. W., & Wu, J. (2008). In search of a missing link. *Knowledge Management*

Howell, A. (2017). Engagement starts at the top: The role of a leader's personality on employee engagement. *Strategic HR Review, 16*(3), 144-146.

Husserl, E. (1927). *Psychological and transcendental phenomenology and the confrontation with Heidegger.* Dordrecht, The Netherlands: Kluwer.

Hunt, J. M., & Weintraub, J. R. (2016). *The coaching manager: Developing top talent in business*. Newbury Park, CA: Sage

Huselid, M. A. (1995). The impact of human resource management practices on turnover, productivity, and corporate financial performance. *Academy of management journal, 38*(3), 635-672.

Ibrahim, A., Soufani, K., & Lam, J. (2003). Family business training: A Canadian perspective. *Education and Training, 45*(9), 474-482.

Jensen, M. C., & Meckling, W. H. (1976). Theory of the firm: Managerial behavior, agency costs and ownership structure. *Journal of Financial Economics, 3*(4), 305-360.

Kahn, W. A. (1990). Psychological conditions of personal engagement and disengagement at work. *Academy of Management Journal, 33*(4), 692-724.

Keller, S., & Price, C. (2011). Organizational health: The ultimate competitive advantage. *McKinsey Quarterly, 2*(6), 94-107.

Kepner, E. (1983). The family and the firm: A coevolutionary perspective. *Organizational Dynamics, 12*(1), 57-70.

Kesner, I. F., & Sebora, T. C. (1994). Executive succession: Past, present & future. *Journal of management, 20*(2), 327-372.

Klein, S. B., Astrachan, J. H., & Smyrnios, K. X. (2005). The F-PEC scale of family influence: Construction, validation, and further implication for theory. *Entrepreneurship Theory and Practice, 29*(3), 321-339.

Lansberg, I. (1988). The succession conspiracy. *Family Business Review, 1*(2), 119-143.

Leib, G., & Zehrer, A. (2018). Intergenerational communication in family firm succession. *Journal of Family Business Management, 8*(1), 75-90

Lester, R.H. and Cannella, A.A. Jr (2006). Inter-organizational familiness: how family firms use interlocking directorates to build community-level social capital. *Entrepreneurship Theory and Practice, 30*(6), 755-775.

Leventhal, G. S. (1980). What should be done with equity theory?. In *Social exchange* (pp. 27-55). Boston, MA: Springer.

Lewis, R. E., & Heckman, R. J. (2006). Talent management: A critical review. *Human resource management review, 16*(2), 139-154.

Luthans, F., & Peterson, S. J. (2002). Employee engagement and manager self-efficacy. *Journal of management development, 21*(5), 376-387.

Macey, W. H., & Schneider, B. (2008). The meaning of employee engagement. *Industrial and Organizational Psychology, 1*(1), 3-30.

Macey, W. H., Schneider, B., Barbera, K. M., & Young, S. A. (2011). *Employee engagement: Tools for analysis, practice, and competitive advantage* (Vol. 31). West Sussex, UK: John Wiley & Sons.

Maietta, R. C. (2008). *Media Review: MAXQDA 2007.* Marburg, Germany: Verbi Software. *Journal of Mixed Methods Research, 2*(2), 193-198.

Malik, A. R., & Singh, P. (2014). High potential programs: Let's hear it for 'B' players. *Human Resource Management Review, 24*(4), 330-346.

Marler, L., Botero, I., & De Massis, A. (2017). Succession-related role transitions in family firms: The impact of proactive personality. *Strategic Issues in the Family Firm, 29*(1), 57-81.

Mathew, T., & Blumentritt, T. (2015). A sequential choice model of family business succesion. *Small Business Economics, 45*(1), 15-37.

Mehrabani, S. E., & Mohamad, N. A. (2011). Succession planning: A necessary process in today's organization. *International Journal of e-Education, e-Business, e-Management and e-Learning, 1*(5), 371.

Michel, A., & Kammerlander, N. (2014). Role and role adjustment of trusted advisors in the family businesses succession planning process - A conceptual model. Presented at 14th international family enterprise research academy (IFERA) annual conference, Lappeenranta, Finland.

Miller, J. J., Grise-Owens, E., Addison, D., Marshall, M., Trabue, D., & Escobar-Ratliff, L. (2016). Planning an organizational wellness initiative at a multi-state social service agency. *Evaluation and Program Planning, 56*(1), 1-10.

Morrison, E. W., & Robinson, S. L. (1997). When employees feel betrayed: A model of how psychological contract violation develops. *Academy of Management Review, 22*(1), 226-256.

Murray, B. (2003). The succession transition process: A longitudinal perspective. *Family Business Review, 16*(1), 17-33.

Mushref, A. M., & Al-jabiri, L. S. (2016). Empirical framework of the relationship between organizational health and strategic performance. *Net Journal of Social Sciences, 5*(1), 1-8.

Myung, J., Loeb, S., & Horng, E. (2011). Tapping the principal pipeline: Identifying talent for future school leadership in the absence of formal succession management programs. *Educational Administration Quarterly, 47*(5), 695-727.

Nosé, L., Korunka, C., Frank, H., & Danes, S. M. (2017). Decreasing the effects of relationship conflict on family businesses. *Journal of Family Issues, 38*(1), 25-51.

Nietzsche, F. (1997). *Untimely meditations.* New York, NY: Cambridge University Press.

Obadan, J. A., & Ohiorenoya, J. O. (2013). Succession planning in small business enterprises in Edo State of Nigeria. *European Scientific Journal, 9*(31), 64-76.

Onwuka, E. M., Onyinye, E., Dibua, E., & Ekene, E. (2017). Succession management and organizational survival in selected transportation companies in Ontisha, Nigeria. *International Journal of Management Sciences and Business Research, 6*(1), 70-83.

Pandita, D., & Ray, S. (2018). Talent management and employee engagement: A meta-analysis of their impact on talent retention. *Industrial and Commercial Training, 50*(4), 185-199.

Papalexandris, N., & Galanaki, E. (2009). Leadership's impact on employee engagement: Differences among entrepreneurs and professional CEOs. *Leadership & Organization Development Journal, 30*(4), 365-385.

Parker, S. K. (1998). Enhancing role breadth self-efficacy: the roles of job enrichment and other organizational interventions. *Journal of Applied Psychology, 83*(6), 835.

Pfeffer, J. (2001). Fighting the war for talent is hazardous to your organization's health. *Organizational Dynamics, 29*(4), 248-259.

Pindado, J., & Requejo, I. (2015). Family business performance from a governance perspective: A review of empirical research. *International Journal of Management Reviews, 17*(3), 279-311.

Prahalad, C. K., & Hamel, G. (2006). The core competence of the corporation. In *Strategische unternehmungsplanung—strategische unternehmungsführung* (pp. 275-292). Berlin, Heidelberg: Springer.

Quinn, J. B., Anderson, P., & Finkelstein, S. (1996). Leveraging intellect. *The Academy of Management Executive, 10*(3), 7-27.

Renkert-Thomas, A. (2016). Alternatives to engaged ownership. In *Engaged ownership: A guide for owners of family businesses* (pp. 105-112). Hoboken, NJ: John Wiley & Sons.

Richards, C. L. (2009). *A new paradigm: Strategies for succession planning in higher education.* Capella University.

Rothwell, W. J. (2010). *Effective succession planning: Ensuring leadership continuity and building talent from within.* New York, NY: American Management Association.

Rothwell, W. J., Jackson, R. D., Ressler, C. L., Jones, M. C., & Brower, M. (2015). *Career planning and succession management: Developing your organization's talent - for today and tomorrow.* Westport, CT: Greenwood Press.

Sale, F. (1987). *Personnel Psychology, 40*(3), 627-630.

Sambrook, S. (2005). Exploring succession planning in small, growing firms. *Journal of Small Business and Enterprise Development, 12*(4), 579-594.

Samei, H., & Feyzbakhsh, A. (2016). The effect of mentoring on successor nurturing in family businesses. *The Journal of Entrepreneurship, 25*(2), 211-231.

Schaubroeck, J., & Jones, J. R. (2000). Antecedents of workplace emotional labor dimensions and moderators of their effects on physical symptoms. *Journal of Organizational Behavior, 21*(2),163-183.

Schulze, W. S., Lubatkin, M. H., Dino, R. N., & Buchholtz, A. K. (2001). Agency relationships in family firms: Theory and evidence. *Organization Science, 12*(2), 99-116.

Seibert, S. E., Kraimer, M. L., & Crant, J. M. (2001). What do proactive people do? A longitudinal model linking proactive personality and career success. *Personnel Psychology, 54*(4), 845-874.

Sharma, P. (2004). An overview of the field of family business studies: Current status and directions for the future. *Family Business Review, 17*(1), 1-36.

Sharma, P., Chrisman, J. J., & Chua, J. H. (2003). Succession planning as planned behavior: Some empirical results. *Family Business Review, 16*(1), 1-15.

Sharma, P., Chrisman, J. J., Pablo, A. L., & Chua, J. H. (2001). Determinants of initial satisfaction with the succession process in family firms: A conceptual model. *Entrepreneurship Theory and Practice, 25*(3), 1-19.

Sharma, P., & Rao, A. S. (2000). Successor attributes in Indian and Canadian family firms: A comparative study. *Family Business Review, 13*(4), 313-330.

Shirley, M. M. (2008). Institutions and development. In *Institutions and Development*. Edward Elgar Publishing.

Shoaf, C., Genaidy, A., Karwowski, W., & Huang, S. H. (March 08, 2005). Improving performance and quality of working life: A model for organizational health assessment in emerging enterprises. *Human Factors and Ergonomics in Manufacturing & Service Industries, 14*(1), 81-95.

Smith, J. A. (2004). Reflecting on the development of interpretative phenomenological analysis and its contribution to qualitative research in psychology. *Qualitative Research in Psychology, 1*(1), 39-54.

Smith, J. A., Flowers, P., & Larkin, M. (2013). *Interpretative phenomenological analysis: theory, method and research*. London, UK: Sage.

Smith, J. A., & Osborn, M. (2015). Interpretative phenomenological analysis as a useful methodology for research on the lived experience of pain. *British journal of pain, 9*(1), 41-42.

Statistics Brain. (2016). Family-owned business statistics. Retrieved from https://www.statisticbrain.com/family-owned-business-statistics/

Stevens, B. (2008). Corporate ethical codes: Effective instruments for influencing behavior. *Journal of Business Ethics, 78*(4), 601-609.

Stewart, A., & Hitt, M. A. (2012). Why can't a family business be more like a nonfamily business? Modes of professionalization in family firms. *Family Business Review, 25*(1), 58-86.

Stewart, L. (2015). Family business advisor training. Lecture presented in Rochester, NY.

Storey, J. and Sission, K. (1993). *Managing human resources and industrial relations.* Buckingham, UK: Open University Press.

Van der Heyde, L., Blondel, C., & Carlock, R. S. (2005). Fair process: Striving for justice in family business. *Family Business Review, 18*(1), 1-21.

Walsh, D. (2010). Regeneration: Those who follow in family footsteps often must set a new pace. *Crain's Detroit Business.* Retrieved from https://www.crainsdetroit.com/article/20100718/C02/307189986/

Wee, Y. G., & Ibrah Wee, Y. G., & Ibrahim, M. D. (2012). Family business success factors: Management practices, relationship among members, and succession experience. *International Journal of Arts and Commerce, 1*(6), 262-274.

Welch, M. (2011). The evolution of the employee engagement concept: Communication implications. *Corporate Communications: An International Journal, 16*(4), 328-346.

Whitehouse, M. (2010). Another threat to economy: Boomers cutting back. *Wall Street Journal, 10,* 41. Retrieved from https://www.wsj.com/articles/SB10001424052748703321004575427881929070948

Young, M. N., Peng, M. W., Ahlstrom, D., Bruton, G. D., & Jiang, Y. (2008). Corporate governance in emerging economies: A review of the principal–principal perspective. *Journal of Management Studies, 45*(1), 196-220.

Zhao, H. A. O., Wayne, S. J., Glibkowski, B. C., & Bravo, J. (2007). The impact of psychological contract breach on work-related outcomes: A meta-analysis. *Personnel Psychology, 60*(3), 647-680.

Printed in the United States
by Baker & Taylor Publisher Services